TRUE STORIES OF GOD'S LEADING
IN SIX GENERATIONS OF ADVENTIST GIRLS

HANNAH'S Girls

Marilla
(1851-1916)

Ruth Vitrano Merkel

REVIEW AND HERALD® PUBLISHING ASSOCIATION
HAGERSTOWN, MD 21740

The Review and Herald Publishing Association publishes biblically-based
materials for spiritual, physical, and mental growth and Christian
discipleship.

The author assumes full responsibility for the accuracy of all facts and
quotations as cited in this book.

This book was
Edited by Penny Estes Wheeler
Designed by Tina M. Ivany
Cover illustration by Matthew Archambault
Electronic makeup by Shirley M. Bolivar
Typeset: Goudy 13/16

PRINTED IN U.S.A.
10 09 08 07 06   5 4 3 2 1

R&H Cataloging Service
Merkel, Ruth Vitrano
    Marilla

    1. Seventh-day Adventists—Biography.   2. Seventh-day Adventists—
History.   I. Title   II. Series: Hannah's Girls

286.73209

ISBN 10: 0-8280-1952-5
ISBN 13: 978-0-8280-1952-1

Dedication

To my daughters,
Elaine and Marcia,
&
To my grandchildren,
Erin, Benjamin, and Bradley

To order additional copies of *Hannah's Girls: Marilla* (Book 2), by Ruth Merkel, call 1-800-765-6955.

Visit us at **www.reviewandherald.com** for information on other Review and Herald® products.

Contents

Introduction

Ann Eddy, of *Hannah's Girls: Ann* (Book 1), is now married and the mother of two daughters, Marilla and Annie Laurie. Life on a farm in northeastern Wisconsin keeps Ann and her daughters busy and happy. Marilla, especially, likes it that good neighbors live only a mile away.

A new teacher and the return of a close girlfriend make Marilla's eighth-grade year very special. Yet terror lurks in the background—battles fought hundred of miles from their happy home shdow even their happiest times.

This true story is Book 2 of a six-book series.

—*Ruth Merkel*

Hannah's Girls Family Tree

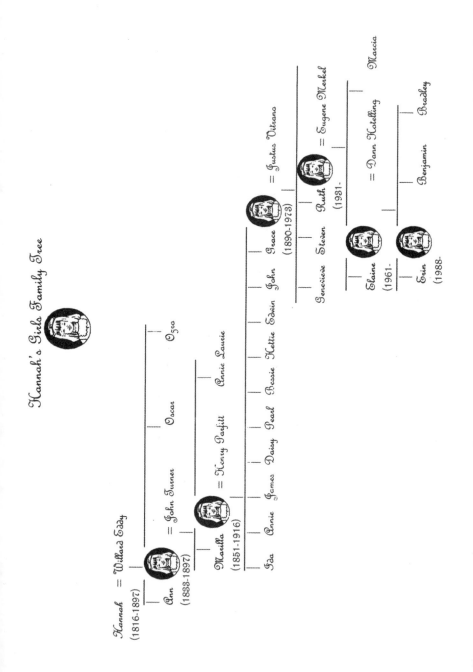

Hannah = Willard Eddy
(1816-1897)

Ann = John Turner
(1888-1897)

Oscar   Osa

Marilla = Henry Padgitt
(1851-1916)

Ida Annie James Daisy Pearl Bessie Hettie Edwin John Grace Annie Laurie
                                                            (1890-1973)

Grace = Justus Vitrano
(1890-1973)

Ruth = Eugene Merkel
(1981-)

Genevieve Steven   Marcia

Elaine = Dann Hotelling
(1961-

Erin   Benjamin   Bradley
(1988-

Generation Two

Marilla
(1851-1916)

ERIN'S GREAT-GREAT-GRANDMOTHER

Some of the people you'll meet in Marilla . . .

MARILLA TURNER: daughter of a Civil War soldier

JOHN (THE SOLDIER), AND HIS WIFE ANN EDDY TURNER:

ANNIE LAURIE: Marilla's little sister

JULIA KELLY: Ann's childhood friend, and her husband, **TIMOTHY**

LUCINDA KELLY: Marilla's best friend

THE OTHER KELLY CHILDREN: Patty Ann, Ethan, and Jared

THE PARFITT FAMILY: Marilla's closest neighbors

THE PARFITT CHILDREN: Henry, Bessie, Joe, Jim, and Austin

EILEEN DONOVAN: Sweet Briar School's teacher

ERIK IVERSEN AND RICHARD LATCHER: eighth-grade classmates of Marilla and "Cinda"

ONE

Best Friends—Again

 It was a picture-perfect Wisconsin summer day, the sun chasing clouds across the sky as a warm breeze stirred the air. Bobolinks sang in the meadow, and meadowlarks serenaded from the fence posts where they perched, looking over their kingdoms. Somewhere a farm dog barked, and another one answered. Dew was still drying in the sun, so here and there the grass sparkled like diamonds.

Marilla loved summer. As she stood on the porch with her little sister, Marilla pulled her long brown hair to the top of her head, smiled at the sky, and sighed. "Isn't it a beautiful day, Annie Laurie? I wish I were a bird flying in that clear, blue sky. How could anywhere be more beautiful than right here in Liberty, Wisconsin. It's going to be a special, exciting day. I can feel it in my soul." Marilla had a way with words. Her mother, Ann Turner, often fondly referred to her as being serenely poetic.

Annie Laurie nodded her agreement. "Let's go swing," she eagerly suggested, tugging on Marilla's hand. "I wanna show you something I can do."

"First let's do our chores. Then we can play."

There was always work to be done on the farm.

Marilla and her sister understood what was expected of them as did all the other farm children in the community. Working hard and carrying and sharing responsibility was the way of life for both young and old.

Slipping the handle of the egg basket over her arm, Marilla called, "I'm going to gather the eggs now, Mama."

"Remember to feed the chickens and see if the tomato plants need some water," Mother reminded her.

So off the sisters went, their devoted dog at their heels.

"I'll feed the dog and cats, 'Rilla, and I'll help you water the tomatoes. Then we'll swing!" The little girl's eyes sparkled with excitement as she ran to the barn.

Being several years older than her sister, Marilla pampered Annie Laurie considerably. *I s'pose she has some new trick to show me,* she thought with a smile.

Opening the door to the hen house, Marilla called to the hen nearest the door, "Get off your nest, Hester. Are you hiding any eggs?" She reached her hand into the nest, felt an egg, grasped it, and carefully placed it in the basket. Hester fussed, clucked, fluffed, and rearranged her white feathers as she settled herself back on her nest.

Marilla collected all the eggs, and then filled a small pail with feed.

"Come, chick-chick-chick! Come, chick-chick-chick!" she trilled, and the chickens came running and clucking as she scattered their feed on the ground.

Dutifully, the girls watered the tomato plants, then took the egg basket to the house. At last they could play. They ran to the old oak tree where their father, John

Turner, had hung a swing from very long ropes tied to a high branch overhead.

"Shall we both get on the swing?" asked Marilla. "I'll stand up, and we'll pump together."

"First let me show you my surprise. Watch!" The little girl grabbed the ropes, ran forward, and jumped up on the wooden seat, pumping for all she was worth.

Marilla sat down on a nearby stump and ran her hand across the grass, inspecting each blade closely. "Ah ha! Here's a four-leaf clover," she said, pinching it from the cluster. "I thought I might spot one."

"Save it for me, I might need it," Annie Laurie called. "Here I go!"

And when the swing was at its highest point, the little girl let go of the ropes and sailed through the air, her brown braids flying, her arms outstretched like a bird, and her eyes shining with delight. Hitting the ground, she dropped, turned a crooked somersault, and rolled to a stop.

"Annie Laurie Turner! You little daredevil!" Marilla cried, jumping up to give her sister a hug. "How athletic you are. Much more than I am."

"But you're better at riding horses," Annie Laurie said honestly.

"Yes, that I am, thanks to Uncle Ozro," laughed Marilla.

"I wish I had Uncle Ozro here to teach me how to ride a horse like he taught you."

"Oh, yes, I wish that too. It would be wonderful if he lived nearby. He could ride like Jehu."

The little girl swung on her sister's hands, pulling her into a twirl. "I love to hear you tell stories about how you and Lucinda Kelly used to race around on your horses with Uncle Ozro. But Mama says I remind her of her brother Oscar. He did stunts and tricks." Annie Laurie dropped Marilla's hands and turned another somersault on the warm grass.

"Yes, Uncle Oscar was a born clown. He could have been a gymnast in a circus, I believe. But Uncle Ozro loved racing with the wind, and he wasn't afraid to stretch his luck. Mama swore he was courting disaster, and Grandma just threw up her hands."

Marilla enjoyed remembering the days when she'd lived just down the road from her uncles and Grandma Hannah Eddy in southern Wisconsin. She only wished she could have known Grandpa Willard, but he had passed away before she was born.

Grabbing the pail her mother had left by the back door, Marilla went to the pump for fresh water. She tried to be careful not to let too much slosh out as she made her way back to the house. It took two hands to carry the heavy bucket, and the few cold drips that sprinkled her legs felt good and refreshing.

"Thanks, Rilla," Mother said as she elbowed open the screen door. Marilla slipped past her and heaved the bucket up on the wooden counter.

"It's such a magnificent morning, Mama. I wish I could do something special, something extraordinary. I wonder what Bessie Parfitt's up to. May I ride over to see her . . . maybe later?"

"Perhaps after your father gets back from New London. He's running errands this morning." Mama was back at the kitchen table, her knuckles deep in the bread dough she was kneading. She gave the mound a punch and a quarter turn, adding almost as an afterthought, "Probably Papa will stop in at Mr. Murphy's print shop to pick up the weekly newspaper, so's he can keep up on the war news."

"He might even run into Uncle Stephen, if he's in town, too," Marilla said. "They'll chat a spell. You know how they do." She paused, and suddenly the air was heavy with the name that neither mentioned. Uncle Charles, Father's other brother, had enlisted in August of 1862 and died hardly four months later as a result of the Battle of Perryville. That battle had saved Kentucky for the Union, but the loss of life on both sides was terrible.

Mother's hands were still, resting upon the floured mound of dough. Her eyes looked out the small kitchen window. "Yes," she said after a pause, "both Papa and Stephen are perturbed and troubled about this Civil War."

"Losing Uncle Charles has been hard on both of them," Marilla noted. "Whenever the topic comes up I see in their faces how they feel the loss, even though it's been two years." She sighed. The whole family still mourned for their lively, cheerful Uncle Charlie.

"I try not to think of it, but it still hurts, doesn't it, Mama?"

"Yes, indeed, daughter, that it does. On the bright side, though, your Uncle Stephen's eye seems to be healing well, and for that we are all thankful. But he may yet lose the sight in it. Antietam was a dreadful battle!" She almost spit out the last words. "But Stephen almost seems determined to rejoin when his eye completely heals and the doctors give their permission."

Marilla closed her eyes, took a deep breath, and shook her head in an attempt to chase the misery of war from her mind.

"I'm awfully glad I've got Bessie to play with," she mused. Bessie, the closest neighbor girl, lived down the road about a mile. When the families first met, the Parfitt family had recently arrived from England and the Turners had moved up from Wheatland. Bessie had one older brother, Henry, and three younger brothers, Joe, Jim, and young Austin who was born just after they'd arrived in America. Even though Bessie was three years older than Marilla, the girls enjoyed being together. Things were always lively, very lively, at the Parfitt home.

Then humming a little tune to herself, she absent-mindedly stepped into the front room and gazed out the window. Suddenly she called excitedly, "Someone's turning in at our place, Mama. Don't recognize who it is, but there's a lady in a wagon, and two girls."

Mother came and stood next to her, wondering who it was.

"Let me see, let me see, too!" Annie Laurie squealed, squeezing between both of them and standing on her tiptoes.

"I don't recognize them either, Rilla, but you go meet them. I'll be right out as soon as I take off my apron."

Ann Turner never wore her kitchen apron when company was around.

"Hello there! This is the Turner place," Marilla cheerily called as she strode toward the wagon. "I'm Marilla. May I help . . . I mean . . ." She gasped. "Why it's Mrs. Kelly! And can that be you, Lucinda?"

"Mama! Mama!" she cried, turning swiftly. "Come quick!"

Ann hurried out with Annie Laurie right behind her.

"Good morning, may I help—" but Mother never finished her greeting. She stopped dead in her tracks as she looked at the visitors with curious regard. Then with a cry of happiness she rushed toward them. "Why, Julia Dunbar . . . Julia Kelly! Is it really you? I haven't seen you in ages!"

"Yes, Ann. Dear, dear Ann. Yes, I'm Julia." The women hugged, laughed, and cried all at the same time, stopping to look at each other, then hugging and laughing again.

Marilla turned to the girls who'd already jumped down from the wagon and were happily watching the delightful reunion.

"Hi, Rilla, I'm so *excited* to see you again." Lucinda was laughing and speaking at the same time. "And look! This is Patty Ann. She was born after you left Wheatland."

"Well how do you do, Patty Ann? I see you have your sister's blond, curly hair, and your mother's green eyes. And this"—she nudged her sister—is my little sister, Annie Laurie. She was born right here in Liberty."

Lucinda gave a slight bow. "Hi, Annie Laurie. That's a beautiful name."

She half turned to glance at her mother. "Isn't it funny to hear our mothers call each other by their maiden names?" she chuckled. "Of course when they first met as young girls on that wagon train back East, they were Julie Dunbar and Ann Eddy. 'Course now that Mother's grown, everyone calls her Julia instead of Julie."

The women were talking so fast they almost interrupted each other.

"What are you doing here, Julia?" Mother asked. "Where's Timothy, that wonderful husband of yours, and those boys?"

"We're moving here. We'll be neighbors again!"

"Here? Here to Liberty? Why . . . uhh . . . how?"

Amazement written all over her face, Marilla turned to her friend. A grinning Lucinda nodded her head in confirmation and grabbed her hand. They did a quick waltz around the yard to celebrate.

Mrs. Kelly explained. "Tim's Uncle Jake deeded a farm to him that's not far from here—over near Mosquito Hill."

"Why you must mean old Dutch Jake's place. I know right where it is. That's wonderful!"

Julia's green eyes sparkled. "Uncle Jake and Aunt Cordelia had no children of their own, and Tim was always a favorite of Uncle Jake's. So they left the farm to him."

Mother couldn't find enough words to express her delight. She and Julia had met years before when they were 10, when their families had traveled by wagon from New York to Wisconsin. When they'd grown up, Julia had married Timothy Kelly and remained in Wheatland. Ann married John Turner, and they'd moved to the New London area with John's brother LeRoy. Since travel wasn't easy, the young families had not seen each other since.

Marilla just couldn't stop smiling. "Come on," she suggested, "let's sit on the porch and talk. We'll never get a word in edgewise here with our mothers jabbering so fast."

Taking Annie Laurie by the hand, Marilla led the way.

"I never thought we'd be neighbors again. Oh, this is marvelous!" she bubbled. "I just knew today was going to be special. I said so when I first got up this morning." She leaned against the warm porch post and raised her arms toward the sky.

"It's really quite remarkable," Lucinda agreed. "Almost miraculous, I'd say. I thought we'd stay in Wheatland forever. But if we had to move, I certainly couldn't have chosen a better place than to be near you. You look just about the same, Rilla, 'cept taller. 'Course, your beautiful eyes haven't changed at all. You know I've always envied them. Mother says your eyes are the color of sapphires."

"Strange twist, isn't it?" Marilla wagged her head with a grin. "Ever since we were little, I've longed to have your wavy hair, and you've admired my eyes. You're even a bit taller than I am, though I'm two weeks older than you are. How dare you?" she laughed.

"Isn't it fun growing up! Ethan teases me that I'm getting old."

"And how are those brothers of yours?" Marilla wondered.

"Ethan and Jared are both fine. They're back at our new house helping Pa unpack. We haven't even had time to completely move in, but Mother insisted that she find you folks immediately. She promised Pa she wouldn't be gone long, but Pa laughed and told her to take her time."

"What do your brothers call you now? 'Cinda' or 'Lu'?" Marilla asked.

Lucinda nodded. "I still go by all three names at home. But I prefer Cinda."

Just then their mothers flew past the girls and into the house on the run. The girls looked at each other and laughed to hear Mother saying, "Oh, Julia, I forgot the bread!"

Cinda nudged Marilla with her elbow. "'Member what fun we had—'specially with your Uncle Ozro teaching us to ride old Dobbin, that wonderful chestnut horse of his— and how our mothers were horrified to see us gallop by."

Marilla nodded. "Annie Laurie and I were talking about just that earlier this morning. I can still see our mothers wringing their hands. I'm sure Mama thought Uncle Ozro was making tomboys out of us, and that he'd get us killed in the process. Annie Laurie wishes so much that he were here to teach her to ride and do some of his tricks."

The Turner's big golden retriever jumped up on the porch to join the happy party. He wagged his tail as he gently licked Cinda's outstretched hand.

Marilla jumped up and draped her arm around the

dog's neck. "This is our dog," she announced. "He likes to meet all our company. Sit, Barkley!" She pointed her finger at the dog.

"Barkley? Barkley! What a clever name for a dog." Cinda threw back her head and laughed.

"Yeah, 'cept he doesn't bark much," said Annie Laurie as the younger girls edged in closer so they could pat his golden neck, too.

"Just think, we'll be in school together, Cinda. Won't that be fun?"

Cinda beamed. "You bet. Mother hoped you'd have a school here in Liberty, and she was so relieved to find that the schoolhouse is nearby. Who'll be in eighth grade with us?"

"Two boys. Richard Latcher and Erik Iversen."

"I hope they're nice fellas."

"Oh, they are. They can tease—like most boys. But they really are fun, and both of them are smart. Richard is polite, kind, smart, and quietly humorous. Erik is cleverly bright and witty, and a good student, too."

Annie Laurie had had enough of talk. "Wanna see our baby kittens?" she interrupted. "They're in the barn. Let's go!" She took off at a trot, and the others followed.

Snuggled down in the straw was the orange and white mother cat with her four kittens. Marilla squatted next to her and spoke softly as she carefully lifted a small, mewing bundle of fur. "Will you let me hold one of your babies, Purrl? I won't hurt it," she murmured. She turned to Cinda. "Its eyes are just beginning to open. See?"

"Oh, how precious," cooed Cinda. "What did I hear you call your cat? Purrl? That's one name I've never heard for a cat." Again she tossed back her hair and laughed with delight.

"Our other cat's named Purrsnikity, but we just call him Purrcy." Marilla's eyes twinkled as she watched Cinda's face for her reaction.

"You're serious, aren't you?" Cinda teased. She took the tiny kitten from her friend's hand and held it to her cheek.

"Mama says my sister's clever with words," Annie Laurie boasted.

"Well, if those are your cats' names, and your dog is Barkley, what on earth do you call your horse?" Cinda pointed to the handsome brown and white horse standing in his stall directly behind Marilla.

The girl grinned and leaned around and up to pat the horse's thigh. "This is Clip. Clop's in town with Papa."

"Clip and Clop. That's too much!" Cinda leaned against the horse's stall and groaned.

Gentle Clip never stopped chewing his oats, but he turned his head toward Marilla and whisked his white tail as if to say, 'I hear you!'

"Let's go swing, Patty Ann," suggested Annie Laurie, never one to sit still for too long. So the two ran off to the old oak tree.

❧

Meanwhile, back in the house, the women were visiting non-stop.

"I was happy to see you have a school here," Julia said, "and so close. Tim and I are pleased. Somehow I worried that way up here in the big woods there might not be a school."

Mother playfully squinted her eyes at her old friend. "Are you implying that we aren't civilized here, Julia?"

"No, but I must admit I wondered. Both Ethan and Jared now prefer to work with their father. They feel they've had enough schooling, and Tim appreciates and needs their help on the farm. Ethan's the one with itchy feet, though. It wouldn't surprise me if he'd find a job in town rather than do farming. But Jared loves farming. Says he never wants to do anything else." She laughed. "But we were talking about a school. I was hoping there'd be a good school here for our girls."

"Let me assure you, my dear friend, that there is. A *good* school. But there was no school at all when we first moved here." She shook her head, remembering. "Early on, John and I decided that if at all possible we'd provide schooling for any children we might have. It was a promise we were determined to keep. We couldn't have it any other way. You remember how I feel about education."

Mrs. Kelly nodded emphatically.

"By the time we moved here I'd already taught Marilla to read, and she was a child who fulfilled my dreams. It seemed that her little mind was a like a sponge—'thirsting for knowledge'—to quote my mother." She laughed, remembering. "Mother felt that Marilla's bright mind should not be neglected, so I wrote to the county superintendent and asked him how I could get a school started."

"The *superintendent*, Ann?" Mrs. Kelly's eyes widened. "What on earth did he say?"

"He told me that he'd arrange for a visit from Abner Haley, a member of the school board, to investigate my inquiry. If he was satisfied that there'd be enough children to fill a school, one could be started.

"He also said that the parents—that was us—would have to furnish five things: the schoolhouse, the desks, the stove, the books, *and* the teacher. The school board would pay the wages, but we had to find her."

"That was a difficult, big order to fill.

"Well, we began talking to the neighbors to get the ball rolling, and to our delight we found that other families were willing to join the venture."

Julia hugged herself, so glad to be back with her old friend. "You could sell ice to an Eskimo, Ann," she laughed.

Mother laughed too. "Maybe so. Anyway, it was your Tim's aunt and uncle—Dutch Jake and Cordelia Stryker— who offered to let us use their old log cabin until a proper school could be built. There was plenty of room on Stryker's land to build a new school, to boot. Cordelia called it the Sweet Briar School, and we all figured she had the right to name it. My, she was a precious lady. Never had any children of her own, but she and Dutch Jake raised two orphan boys. It goes to show you what good people they were."

"I never knew them, but Tim says his aunt and uncle were jewels. Tell me more about the school. I can't believe it was easy."

Mother leaned back, ready to tell the story. It had taken a lot of determination and tenacity to get the school going. Five families had joined them in the quest. "Six counting us," she said. "They were the Latchers, Iversens, Zimmermans, the Phelps, and the Parfitts."

Mrs. Kelly listened attentively. These folks would be her neighbors.

"We all scrubbed and scraped in our spare time, if there was such a thing. But you know the old saying that many hands make light work. It's true! 'Course, now we have the new building."

"You're speaking of the nice school on the corner near us?"

Mother nodded. "Mr. Iversen's a fine carpenter, and he offered to make the benches and desks. Mr. Latcher helped him. Mrs. Iversen was so excited about the prospect of a school that she went down every so often to sweep and clean the old place up—yard and all. She cut down the scraggly shrubs and the thicket, and she planted daffodil bulbs as well as lilac bushes that are just gorgeous every spring.

"The Zimmermans donated an old, but dependable stove, and Clayton Phelps and my John did the masonry work to get the old chimney workable and safe. We replaced some broken window panes, too.

"Clay and his wife, Libby, surprised us all when they hung a large, framed portrait of George Washington on the wall of that old schoolhouse the very first day school began. I couldn't help but get tears in my eyes when I saw it."

Mother paused. "It seemed like the perfect finishing touch.

"Well, the Parfitts furnished the blackboard. Henry, Bessie, and Joe are finished with their schooling now, but Jim still attends. Henry is the oldest of all our community children, and he was more interested in learning things from the Indians upriver than in learning things in school. He could already read, write, and do good arithmetic anyway. That boy, I tell you, is remarkably bright. He is friends with the local Indians, and they like him too."

"We ran into Henry just before coming to see you," Julia told her. "He was going by on the road and stopped to greet us. He introduced himself and offered to help. The boys took to him immediately. He seems capable and has a nice way about him."

Mother agreed. Henry did have a nice way about him. "John always says that he's a true English gentleman, the same as his father. You'll enjoy meeting the Parfitts, Julia. They're quality folks."

"It seems to be that you're the true reason we have this school," Julia said, fanning away flies with her hand. "I thank you!"

Mother accepted her thanks but quickly added that the Widow Dexter was the one who'd found their first teacher. A friend of hers had recommended a bright young woman from Waupaca who was willing to move to their area—Miss Lorena Appleby. As soon as he interviewed her, the county superintendent had given her a teaching permit. It seemed providential how everything had worked together.

Of course, some in the community didn't approve or even care one way of the other. "There were the nay-sayers," Mother said, "who took no interest at all in the project." The Endicotts, the Blairs, and Otis and Halie Bunker thought that a school was unnecessary. It wasn't that they objected, but they just didn't raise a finger to help. "'Twas a pity young Willy Bunker didn't get any schooling," Mother added. "He probably could've amounted to something. Got shot to death in a drunken brawl in Green Bay."

Julia sighed. It almost seemed impossible that such a thing could happen in such a beautiful place and with such nice folks. "How old was the boy when he died?"

"Almost 20. Much too young!" Mother shook her head. This tragedy still touched her heart. "It's a puzzle why some youngsters are hell-bent on being bad."

Changing the subject, she continued with her story. Each of the families supporting the school had donated money to buy school books. When the superintendent visited the new Sweet Briar School he approved everything they'd done. The school opened that fall and that first year, under Miss Appleby's guidance, Marilla completed two grades. Miss Appleby taught for six years, but just this summer she'd married a local fellow, Palmer Crockett. Now a new teacher was coming from Boston— Miss Eileen Donovan. "At least we hope she comes," Mother said. "One of Pastor Burlingame's relatives from Oshkosh wrote to Eileen about our opening. We understand that she's applied for the teaching position."

"It seems that teaching is often a stepping-stone to marriage," Mrs. Kelly said with a laugh.

"You're right about that. Farmers and villagers alike seem to prize teachers," agreed Mother. "But that's to be expected. I'd think that any woman who's educated, independent, and good with kids would make a fine wife. It's the men who have to prove themselves to win their hearts."

Julia clapped her hands and laughed at that. Her old friend Ann hadn't changed.

The women enjoyed each other, just as they'd done in the old days. By now the bread dough had risen, so Mother got up to shape it into loaves. It wouldn't take long in the summer heat to rise again. Now the old friends strolled arm in arm back to Julia's wagon. The girls returned from another look at the kittens. It was obvious that they'd had fun jumping in the haymow, too, for they were shaking straw from their hair. As usual, Barkley tagged along, his tail wagging joyfully.

"Well, we'd better start back," Mrs. Kelly told her daughters.

"Do we have to?" Cinda asked.

"Yes, or your father will think we're lost."

"Tell Tim that we're so happy to have you here," Mother said, giving Julia a hug. "John will be around to see him shortly—probably as soon as he gets home from town."

Cinda flung her arm around Marilla's shoulders.

"Bye! Come see us soon," called Patty Ann as she climbed into the wagon. Annie Laurie waved, then lifted Barkley's paw in a doggie-wave, too.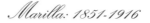

TWO

Always a Picnic at the Parfitts

 In no time—and with a little help from the Turners—the Kellys settled into their new home. And at church the very next Sunday, Pastor Burlingame officially introduced the new family. Of course, the Kellys were warm, out-going people so the bridge of friendship was easily crossed.

There was more good news too. Miss Eileen Donovan had, indeed, been approved and accepted by the county board of education. "She comes with excellent recommendations," the pastor said. "She has a certificate stating she has graduated in arithmetic, grammar, composition, geography, history, botany, and art."

The parishioners looked at each other, murmuring their pleasure, while the children poked one another and whispered in excitement.

It was a Sunday of surprises, for next Pastor Burlingame asked "our friends, the Graybulls" to stand. Flint and Maude quickly stood, smiling at those they knew in the pews around them. Cody and Cora had to be urged to stand, and Cody hid his face against his father's jacket. The family was moving to Liberty, the pastor announced. "Flint tells me that they will attend our Liberty

Church," he said, adding formally, "for that we are grateful. Liberty is a growing community and so is our membership. I'm proud of our parish."

"Amen!

"Amen. Amen."

Smiles and words of approval went through the congregation.

Everyone knew Flint. He had a personality you didn't forget, and he'd expanded the fur trading post his great grandfather, Chief Graybull, had established many years before. Flint had done well financially by turning the trading post into a well-managed hardware-type store, selling tools, utensils, guns, and equipment of all kinds. His building also housed the New London post office run by his wife, Postmistress Maude.

The Graybulls had recently purchased the old Logan house in Liberty, giving it new shutters, a new roof, and a new paint job. In their advanced years, the elderly Logans had found themselves unable to keep up their home so had moved to their daughter's home in New London.

When the elder Logans gave up housekeeping, they'd graciously donated their old piano to the new Liberty School. Everyone was delighted. The piano was in good condition, and only needed tuning.

When the pastor announced that the Graybull's were joining their church, Marilla saw Henry give his brother Joe a poke in the ribs. She swallowed a smile at that. Flint enjoyed bragging boisterously about his 'truly American mixed heritage' for he was one-quarter Indian, one-quarter

German, and half Scottish. Just for fun, he'd occasionally wear an old Indian feathered headdress in the store. No one knew who he'd inherited it from, but it didn't matter. It amused the children, and even the grownups smiled when they saw Flint decked out in the ornate piece made with 10 eagle feathers and three rattlesnake tails. Around his neck he'd wear a necklace of bear claws and bone earrings. To top it all off, sometimes he'd jokingly chant and dance around in a circle. The children loved it, and doubling over with laughter, they would try to copy his intricate steps.

Adults laughed too. "Whatcha doin' Flint? A war dance or a Scottish Reel?" the men would tease, caught up in the fun.

The area Indians liked Flint, too. His store was a pleasant meeting place for Flint was able to bridge the gap between the White and Native cultures. During conversations, he would try to explain to the customers that within the Indian tradition, no one would ever be able to understand or accept the idea that a king 3,000 miles away had given the entire country's midsection to another king who was also 3,000 miles away. And now the original settlers—the Indians—were expected to make room for the strangers that were moving in.

"You also must realize what the Indians experienced," Flint explained. "They had to jump from the Stone Age into the industrial age mighty fast." The folks understood his point.

Ever since she was little, Marilla always liked to ride to town with her father when he was going to Flint's trading post. Besides seeing what Flint might have or do, there was Mr. Bradley's blacksmith's shop right next door where things were always noisy and fascinating.

Marilla liked hearing her mother tell of her own father's blacksmith shop in New York, and whenever Marilla watched Mr. Bradley do his work, she'd pretend she was watching her own grandfather.

"It's fun to watch Mr. Bradley bang his hammer on the anvil and put hot metal in cold water and hear it sizzle," Marilla had told her mother. "But it looks dangerous, too, with that roaring furnace."

Her mother agreed. "Yes, a blacksmith must take great care. That's why he wears a leather bib apron to protect him from the hot, flying sparks."

"Once Grandma Hannah told me that blacksmiths are important workers in their communities," Marilla mused. "They make things we need every day such as nails, hinges, and rims for wagon wheels. It's too bad that I never knew Grandpa Willard."

"Your grandma was right. What would we do without blacksmiths? There was always someone in my father's shop. People stopped by just to say 'hello,' if for no other reason. And remember, blacksmiths make horseshoes, too. Your Uncle Oscar learned to shoe horses when he was a young boy back in New York." Mother had smiled just remembering the long ago.

One lazy, hot summer afternoon, Cinda came to visit

Marilla, riding on her handsome tan pony. Of course, Marilla was excited to see her.

"Phew, it's hot," Cinda said, pushing back her sunbonnet and brushing her hair from her forehead. "Mother said I could take some time off so I rode here to see if you're miserably hot, too."

"It's *awful*," Marilla agreed. "Let's go wading in the river. I'll check with Mama. I've already finished my chores," she called over her should as she dashed into the house.

"Where do you plan to wade?" Mother asked.

"I'm going to go see if Bessie will go down to the bayou with us."

Mother stepped onto the small stoop just outside the door and waved at Cinda. Her face was red with sun and sweat, and Marilla looked the same. "All right, you may go as long as Eliza approves. But be careful of the sturgeon," she warned, a twinkle in her eyes. Cinda looked bewildered when Marilla gave her mother a smirk of a smile in reply.

"It's a long story, but you'll hear all about it, I'm sure," Marilla laughed as she jumped up behind Cinda. "Nice pony," she added, giving his rump a pat.

"Grandpa Kelly gave him to us. His name is Corkie, named after Cork, Ireland where Grandpa was born."

"Seems like old times—riding double, doesn't it? Now if we only had Uncle Ozro here to race with us," Marilla sighed.

"He was great fun," Cinda agreed enthusiastically.

Just then Annie Laurie came round the corner of the

barn riding on her pet calf, a light-brown and white Guernsey. She waved a lively greeting to the girls and hollered, "Where ya goin'?"

"Over to the Parfitts," Marilla called back.

"Say hi to everyone for me, and tell Jimmie I'll do a calf race with him any day he chooses, and I'll win!" Annie Laurie shouted.

The two girls laughed as they rode off. "She is energetic, isn't she!" Cinda said with amazement."

"She certainly is," Marilla agreed. "You should see her fly through the air when she jumps from the swing. She pumps the swing up high, lickety split, and then leaps through the air like a bird. Mama has to look the other way."

"Riding calves is a cute trick, too."

"Yeah, she chose little Dotty as her own baby calf right after it was born. She doesn't ride it all the time, but she has fun when she does."

"Dotty's a clever name. I can see why she chose it."

Marilla laughed. "Those white markings on its fawn-brown coat are smaller than usual for a Guernsey, so Annie Laurie named it, 'Dotty.' Some stretch of the imagination, I know!"

"You Turner girls have fun naming your pets don't you?" Cinda grinned over her shoulder at Marilla as she asked, "Now, just what was your mother referring to about the sturgeon?"

Marilla clutched Cinda around the waist as the pony started to trot. "I'll have Bessie tell you about it. She delights in entertaining people with her fish story."

The Parfitt home stood about a mile down the road from the Turners', near the bank of the Wolf River. The bayou area was a good place to sit and dangle your feet or to wade on a hot day.

Marilla often went to the Parfitts, on errands or to play with Bessie. Slightly built, Bess was a lively, spirited girl with dancing eyes and wavy hair that she kept cut short—when almost all girls wore long hair—because she couldn't be bothered, as she said, fussing with it. The Parfitt parents still had their British accents and Marilla loved to hear them speak. The children spoke with slight British accents, too.

"You'll love getting better acquainted with Bessie," Marilla told Cinda as they trotted along. "She thinks of everything! It's like a picnic every time I visit her and her brothers. Something is always brewing at their place."

"From what I've seen so far, I can believe that," Cinda agreed, nodding her curly blond head. "My brothers have gotten acquainted with the Parfitt boys. They seem about as lively as the Kelly boys—and *that's* lively! They like Henry. How old is Henry, anyway? About 16?"

"Yeah. He's a year older than Bessie. We kids all kind of look up to Henry. You probably will, too, when you get to know him."

"He's rather good looking, I think." She paused. His brothers are, too."

"Henry's special, though, at least as far as I'm concerned," Marilla said. "Joe and Jim are both good kids and

little Austin is a sweet boy, if somewhat spoiled. He was born just after the family arrived from England."

Soon they could see the round top of Parfitt's silo shining in the sunshine. Henry and Joe were out in the yard and waved a welcome.

As they trotted closer, Henry teasingly called, "Hey, there! Are you coming to see me, girls?"

Hearing his voice, Bessie came out of the house. "Oh, go on, Henry. No one comes to see *you*," she snickered. They loved to badger each other.

Henry patted the pony's neck with obvious admiration and tied him to the hitching post.

Bessie greeted the girls with a bright smile. "Hot out, isn't it? But I love summer. What's up? Whatever it is, I'm in on it."

"We thought it would be fun to wade in the bayou for a while," Marilla told her. "Cinda's never done it. Do you want to join us? See if your mother will give us permission."

But just then Mrs. Parfitt came to the porch. "Good afternoon, young ladies. Fine day, isn't it?" She smiled graciously. Eliza Parfitt was petite, soft-spoken, and refined. Her manners were impeccable. The local folks all admired and respected her.

"Can we go wading in the bayou, Mother . . . just for a little while?" Bessie asked.

"Why, I see no reason why you *may* not," corrected Mrs. Parfitt, who was particular about grammar. "Yes, you may, Bessie, dear." Her bright smile reached all three girls. "Have you put the dishes away yet, Bessie?"

"Be with you in a jiffy," Bessie called as she ran back into the house to finish her chores.

Turning to her guests, Mrs. Parfitt asked, "How's your mother, Marilla, and yours, too, Cinda?"

Both girls nodded politely and said that their mothers were fine.

"Bessie's not the one to go wading with," warned Henry with a grin. "She's a bit daring in the water." He winked dramatically at Marilla.

"Aw, come now, Henry," defended Marilla. "She doesn't take any chances that are dangerous—at least not anymore!"

"What are you both talking about?" Cinda demanded, sensing a story and not liking being left out on the fun.

Mrs. Parfitt laughed. "You'd better let Bessie tell you about her wading exploits, Cinda. In all probability, Henry would exaggerate. Actually, Bess is very careful around water. I trust her."

"Hi, Rilla and Cinda. What 'cha here for?" Jim came from the barn, little brother Austin tagging half a step behind.

"My dear young man, that's not a very polite question to ask of visitors the moment they arrive," his mother said, ruffling Jim's hair and lovingly patting his back. "Why not inquire as to their health and well-being?" Good manners were expected of the Parfitt children.

"How are you?" responded Jim with a laugh and a low bow. Austin bowed, too, with a cute grin on his always-happy face.

"Let's go!" said Bessie, running out of the house and the girls took off, leaving the boys behind.

Sitting on the bank, the girls took off their shoes and socks. Then, pulling their dresses up to their knees, they eased themselves into the water and began to slowly walk around, enjoying the coolness.

"Doesn't this feel good?" Bessie held up the hem of her skirt in one hand and splashed water on her face with the other.

Her friends agreed. For a while the three just stood still, indulging themselves in the delightfully cool water. Dragonflies with their translucent wings buzzed and hovered just out of reach. Small water bugs skated on the water's surface, while an occasional fish tickled unfamiliar knees.

"Ooooo," murmured Cinda, "this is pure luxury." She lifted her skirt a fraction higher and took a step forward. The water felt *soooo* good. "Back in Wheatland we all learned to swim in Grandpa Kelly's pond," she added. "Mother saw to that. Her own mother—my grandma— and a little brother had drowned, so Mama made sure all her children could swim."

"What a tragedy." Bessie frowned with sympathy. "As much misery as my brothers cause me, I certainly wouldn't want to lose any one of them." She laughed. "Come to think of it, though—Henry could go first!" Bessie was being silly, and her friends knew it. They all laughed together.

"What's this I hear about your dangerous adventure in the river, Bessie?" Cinda was still curious.

"Aaw, it's not a big story, but I still get teased a lot about it."

"It is, too, a big story, Bessie," laughed Marilla. "It's an unbelievably big story, and you know it. I get goose bumps every time I hear it."

"OK," Bessie said. She trailed her fingers through the water then flicked the droplets on her face. "I'll tell you."

It happened on a warm day shortly after they'd moved to Wisconsin. Bessie and Henry had come down to this very river. They were just little kids, but back in England they'd often waded in the small bubbling brook that ran in front of Squire Ernst's estate where they lived. They weren't afraid of the water, but they'd had no experience with a river such as this one. Then as they slowly walked through the water they saw some very big fish swim by.

"We'd never seen sturgeon before, and we were excited about the way they'd swim right next to us," Bessie said. "They didn't seem to be bothered by us. Wow, were they big—about five feet long, maybe longer—at least longer than I was tall." She held her hands far apart to demonstrate their length.

"You're kidding? Right?" Cinda asked. "How could fish that big be in this river?"

"I don't know how. They just were! They were beautiful, actually. Their scales reflected the sunlight as they shimmered past us. After a few went skimming by, I reached out and touched one," Bessie said. "It didn't seem to be annoyed. It just kept on swimming.

"When Henry saw that I'd touched one, he did the

same. We were laughing and splashing, when a huge sturgeon came slithering by right close. I don't know what possessed me, but I grabbed him by the gills and jumped on—just like you'd straddle a horse."

Cinda gasped. "Do you think we'll see some sturgeon today?"

"Naw, probably not. They're not spawning now." Bessie half turned to face the girls but seemed to stumble, and fell to her knees in the water. Marilla reached out to give Bessie a hand, but with a twinkle in her eyes, Bess pulled Marilla down next to her.

"Bess—you rascal! You did that on purpose. You didn't really fall," Marilla laughingly protested, now sitting on the silty river bottom.

"Feels marvelous, doesn't it, Marilla?" teased Bessie as her skirt floated to the surface. She patted it down. "I think Cinda ought to have the same wonderful experience." Bess splashed water toward Cinda and, of course, Cinda splashed her back. Then with a squeal, Cinda "accidentally" slipped. By then they were all laughing so hard they couldn't stand up if they'd tried. They teased and played until they were thoroughly soaked, then finally crawled out to sit on the bank and dry in the hot, golden sun.

The girls wrung the water out their skirts. "Bessie, that was fun!" Cinda giggled. "Marilla said it's always like coming to a picnic to visit you. So, go on, finish your story. What happened after you straddled the sturgeon?"

Bessie lay back against the warm grass, her hands under her head. Closing her eyes against the sun, she continued.

"The fish swam slowly at first, and I thought it was great having a free ride. Then he took off across the bayou. Henry had been hollering, 'Let go! Let go!' but the next thing I heard was him yelling, 'Hang on! Hang on!' I was confused and scared, and I truly did hang on for dear life. I didn't know what was going to happen. When we reached the opposite bank over there—" she motioned with one arm—"the fish turned quickly to recross the bayou. I could see Henry back on the bank, waving his arms and jumping up and down. I really think he was cheering!"

"I *was* cheering."

Bessie jumped up at the sound of her brother's voice.

Henry had quietly sneaked up behind the girls, Joe and Jim with him. "You looked so funny," Henry told her. "Your eyes were bulging and your mouth was wide open, but you weren't making a sound."

"Oh, go away!" Bessie's eyes sparkled.

The boys sat down and Jim coaxed Bessie to continue. He never tired of hearing the story about his big sister.

"Even now, after all these years," Jim said, "other kids still talk about Bessie's famous adventure. I feel as important as Pastor Burlingame whenever I'm asked about it."

Bessie tapped his leg with one toe. "Cinda, you won't believe what happened next," she said. "That fish decided to take a dive. Before I knew it, my head was under water. I thought I was going to drown. But when he came up again I could feel the ground under my feet. There was Henry next to me, pulling me off the fish's back and help-

ing me up the bank. Water was running down my face. I was blinking my eyes trying to see, and shaking my dripping hair out of my face. We sat down—well, I *collapsed*—on the bank is a better way to put it."

Bessie looked at Henry. "It was over in a flash, but while it was happening it seemed like an eternity."

Henry nodded. "After we caught our breath, I began to laugh, and poor Bessie began to cry. That is, I laughed until I looked up and saw Mother standing over us, glaring as only she can when she's perturbed.

"We were so scared. I was sure we'd get the spankings of our lives. Mother is very prim, proper, and petite—as Father says—but small as she is, she can give a right, smart flogging. We don't call her the Yeoman of the Guard for nothing," he added, and the Parfitt children all laughingly agreed.

"The *what?*" Cinda's eyes were wide.

"The Queen's guards at the Tower of London are yeomen of the royal guard. They're called, Beefeaters. They're very stately men," Henry explained. "They wear the old Tudor costumes—red jackets, black, fluffy, tall hats. Squire Ernst had a painting of them, and I always liked looking at it. We children think Mother must have taken training from the Yeoman. Right, Bessie?"

Henry looked at his sister.

"Right!" she replied with a grin. "The Beefeaters are impressive, and so is Mother. Specially when she's perturbed or upset."

"Well," Henry continued, "we did our best to explain

to Mother just what had happened to Bessie. She could see we were quite shaken. She helped us both up, and told us to get into the house and change into dry clothes, and then come back to her immediately—that she wasn't finished talking to us. We knew what that meant."

Bessie nodded and rolled her eyes.

Cinda gazed at Bessie in disbelief. "I'd think you were making this up if it weren't for Marilla, here, and her mother, and for your own mother saying that you should be the one to tell me the story. Did you get taken to the woodshed like you feared?"

"No, by the time we changed our clothes, Mother was over her initial shock. She asked me again to tell her exactly what I'd done, and when I finished stuttering out the story as best I could she sat still a minute, but then started to laugh. She threw up her hands, threw back her head, and laughed. I was so relieved to see she wasn't going to behead me that I started to cry—again."

Henry nodded. "Father came in, and when Mother told him what had happened, he glared, but his eyes twinkled. First he glared at Bessie, then at me. Then he went over to Bessie and hugged her, and he hugged me, too. Mother started crying that she could have lost two children—both at once.

"Father gave us a lecture, of course. Said he didn't bring us here all the way from England just to lose us. 'Course, we almost lost Joe in the Atlantic Ocean while sailing to America."

"*What!*" Cinda sputtered.

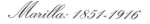

"That's quite another story, Cinda," Bessie interjected. "Young Joe was running on the deck of the ship. He was wearing one of those loose smock tops, you know—like a little girl's dress that little boys wear. Anyway, he was near the railing, and when the ship tossed, he fell and would have rolled off, 'cept Mother grabbed him by his smock and saved his life."

"Good thing I was dressed like a girl, or I wouldn't be here now," Joe said with a bow.

"And such a pity that would be," teased Bessie.

Joe yanked up a handful of grass and threw it at his sister. "See how quickly I'll help you churn butter next time, Bess," he teased.

"I saw Joe fall, too," Henry said, nodding his head. "We could hardly breathe, even after we knew he was safe. Either Father carried him or Mother held his hand all the rest of the day, never letting him out of their sight. Truth is, we kids didn't let him out of our sight either."

Shaking her head, Cinda said, *"And may the saints presairve ye!"*

Everyone laughed with her.

"Hey, you're good," Joe complimented.

"Well, I've heard my Irish Grandpa Kelly's brogue all my life," she said, giving the word 'brogue' an Irish sound. "Do *all* you Parfitts have hair-raising things happen to you? My family has been drab by comparison. Even my horse racing with Rilla's Uncle Ozro in our death-defying gallops doesn't compare to these escapades. You must have had nightmares for a week, Bessie."

"More like a month!"

Marilla smiled. "I told you, Cinda, it's like a picnic being with the Parfitts."

"A picnic! A picnic?" questioned Henry with a grin. "It's no picnic around here, although we do have fun, I'll admit. But we most certainly work hard. Very hard." He moaned, drawing down the corners of his mouth, but his twinkling eyes gave him away.

"I said nothing about your work habits, Henry. I just told Cinda I liked coming here and being with all of you." Marilla looked down her nose at him as she faked an apology with a grin.

"I rather like picnics, myself," Bessie pronounced cheerfully.

"So Joe almost falls overboard, and Bessie almost drowns. Those experiences are far beyond 'picnics,'" Cinda laughed. The others' delighted laughter joined hers, Bessie laughing the loudest of all.

"Go on," Cinda gasped. "Your father didn't get out his leather belt?"

"No, he didn't." Henry shook his head. "I was never so surprised in my life that we didn't get a whipping for our foolishness. But Father said we'd been punished enough already—bein' so scared and all. And I'll have to agree. I was good and scared. I thought Bessie was a goner when I saw her go under the water. I didn't know where that fish was going to come up."

"Faith, and ye'll niver forget that day, will ye now? What a story. It's a miracle Bessie's here to tell about it," Cinda

declared. "I'd say a guardian angel was busy that day."

"Just like the children of Israel going safely through the Red Sea, right?" Jim asked.

They all nodded, agreeing with his comparison.

Marilla turned to Cinda. "Whenever I think of this experience, Isaiah 43:2 comes to my mind. You know, 'When thou passeth through the waters . . . they shall not overflow thee.'"

Cinda nodded her silent assent.

"That's a great promise," Henry said. "I've never forgotten it, not since I first heard you say it." His eyes had a soft shine when he looked at Marilla. "It's a text that brings comfort. God was with us on that awful day when we were just young 'uns, but I think it could tell us that God is close, no matter what trouble we're in."

The little group sat in silence, each pondering the providence of God. A breeze rustled the dry grass. Nearby, a meadowlark trilled. "Well," Henry said, "that wraps up Bessie's first chapter. Do you want her to make up another story?" He ducked his head just as his sister took a swing at him.

"You're too miserable to call a brother," she laughed, turning around at the soft sound of footsteps.

It was Eliza Parfitt sauntering down to the river bank to join the youngsters. Austin was right on her heels.

"Come on back to the house," she told them. "Let's have some cool raspberry drink."

"I helped make it," Austin boasted. "I stirred the pitcher."

Hands under Austin's arms, Henry lifted him in a high arc and swung him around in a wide circle. Austin squealed and giggled, "More, more, Henry. Swing me some more!"

It was obvious that Henry was devoted to young Austin, and that Austin adored his big brother.

❧

July 4 was a great day of celebration in New London. This year the Turners, the Parfitts, and the Kellys all got up early, milked their cows and let them out in their fields, fed the chickens and did other chores, packed lunches, and hurried into their wagons for the trip to town. Everyone wanted to be there when the band played to officially start the picnic. There were ceremonies and holiday fun.

There were organized games for the children and games of horseshoes for the men. Small boys shot off fire crackers; dogs ran and barked. At noon the big shiny church bells sang out to quiet the crowd for grace before eating. And when everyone had eaten all they could hold, the women stood up and shook the crumbs out of the tablecloths. Everyone knew what would happen next.

A platform trimmed with banners had been built in front of city hall, and now lively band tunes drew a crowd to hear speeches by the mayor and the school principal. The War of the Rebellion—now in its third year—was in the minds of everyone there. It had been in the yard of this very city hall, when she was 10, that Marilla's Uncle Stephen had marched with the other volunteers, and gone to war. It had seemed kind of exciting back then. The band played, and there'd been speeches and singing, hugging and crying. But then the families went home while the new soldiers went . . . someplace else. That part was still confusing. Where did they do this fighting anyway? Back then she hadn't understood it at all. Today, she decided not to think about it. At least not for now.

Austin sat on Henry's shoulders so he could see over the people. He liked the band and hummed along with the music, but after the first man had talked for five minutes Austin's kicking feet let Henry know he was bored. "Let's go over to the train station," Henry told his little brother. "The engineer likes to show off for the kids."

Henry wriggled his way through the crowd, Austin still on his shoulders. "Where ya going?" Jim asked, and Henry told him. Jim fell into step behind Henry, and other children quickly joined them. Youngsters running and wrestling in the open field beyond the courthouse, came too. The happy group got to the train station just in time to hear Mr. Hancock sound a high, shrill whistle and clang the shiny bell. White clouds of steam hissed ferociously. The big black engine was spanking clean and gleamed in the bright sunshine. A funny-looking cow catcher jutted out on the front of it. Henry swung Austin to the ground so he could measure himself against the huge wheels. The children laughed when Henry stood against the wheels too. They'd towered over Austin, but Henry was taller than the wheels.

When the speeches were over Henry led his troop of

children back to their parents. A pack of boys went off to play catch, but Marilla, Cinda, and Bessie took Annie Laurie, Patty Ann, and Austin to get ice cream.

A man wearing a red-stripped apron stood scooping it out of a tub that sat in another tub of ice. "Better eat it fast," Bessie told them. "This'll melt in no time." The little girls nodded soberly and bent over their dishes, but Austin gave his sister a grin. "I love ice cream!" he announced.

Ice cream was a real treat. In the summertime the only ice around had been cut from frozen lakes the past winter, packed in sawdust, and stored in ice houses. Even the older girls couldn't help licking the last little bit from their spoons. "When I grow up I'm going to have ice cream every day," Patty Ann sighed.

"Me, too!" the little ones echoed.

"Us, too!" the older ones chorused.

༺ঙ৵ঌ༻

Their ice cream finished, the girls lazily meandered back toward where they'd left their parents, calling the little ones to come too. It felt good to be ladies of leisure, no chores waiting to be finished. Just then two New London girls approached, giggling and whispering to each other under their ruffled summer parasols.

"Hello, Bessie," said the taller girl, Nettie Cameron, in a sing-song voice. "Haven't seen you for a while."

"Hi, Nettie. Hi, Susanna," Bessie replied. Though the speaker had stopped, Bessie kept walking with her friends.

49

"Hey, Bessie," Nettie called coyly. "How's that big brother of yours doing?"

"Oh, he's fine," Bessie said, barely looking over her shoulder. "See ya!"

Taking first Marilla's and then Cinda's arm, Bessie urged them away. The young children scampered ahead of them.

"Who are those girls?" Cinda whispered.

"Just two stuck up girls," was Bessie's impatient answer. "They only talk to people if they're obliged to or care to. Otherwise, they're too busy to give you the time of day."

Cinda twisted around for another look. "They surely are dressed up for a picnic," she observed. "What are their names?"

So Bessie and Marilla explained that Nettie was the daughter of Beulah and Elmer Cameron who owned a cheese factory in town. Susanna was the daughter of Murray Woodruff who worked for the railroad. Mrs. Woodruff had passed away when Susanna was a little girl and her father had not remarried. He was very caring of his only daughter but at the same time—being a gentle, rather quiet man himself—he never encouraged or advised her in matters of social behavior or conduct. He gave her pretty clothes and a loving, warm, beautiful home. They had a housekeeper who helped keep everything clean and nice, and who watched after Susanna. Nettie claimed Susanna as her best friend—at least they were usually together. The choosing was all Nettie's.

As they talked, Maureen Murphy—another New London girl—came toward them. Her face was wreathed with a wide smile. Whenever they met in town both Marilla and Bessie enjoyed Maureen's company. Her father owned and operated a small print company that published a weekly newspaper. The Murphy family was well liked, and of their seven children, Marilla knew the two youngest the best—Pat and Maureen.

"Well, how are the Liberty girls? And who's this?" Maureen smiled directly at Cinda.

Marilla did the introducing and explained to Cinda, "Most of us call this clever girl, Mo. Her little brother came up with that name when he couldn't pronounce Maureen. Somehow it stuck. Right, Mo?"

"Exactly!" Maureen said with a grin. "You may call me Maureen or Mo. I answer to both." She'd obviously seen the girls' previous encounter and said, "Did I see Nettie and Susanna speaking to you, Bessie? Aren't you lucky today!" Maureen's eyes twinkled at Cinda. "All too soon you'll get their number."

"I know how you admire them, Mo," laughed Bessie with a teasing grin. "I'm glad I don't live here in New London and have to see them on a daily basis as you do."

"What makes them waltz around so importantlike, anyway?" Cinda asked.

"Well, I'll tell you," answered Maureen. "You're new here, but you'll soon see that Nettie calls the shots and Susanna walks in her shadow. Susanna is much nicer, and she's prettier than Nettie. I just wish she'd just stand up for herself once in a while. The only reason Nettie attaches herself to Susanna is because Mr. Woodruff is more educated and makes more money than Mr. Cameron, although Mrs. Cameron came from a family of means, as my mother says. Nettie and her older sister, Eulalie, are two of a kind—spoiled rotten."

"That's rather harsh, Mo," Marilla said. She shrugged her shoulders, adding, "but I guess you've pretty well sized up the situation."

Bessie agreed. "Another thing you'll soon learn, Cinda, is that Maureen Murphy marches to her own drummer and isn't intimidated by anyone."

At that, Maureen comically curtsied.

"I'm serious, Mo. I admire your independence and backbone. Those girls get my goat."

"Sometimes you're downright horrible, Bessie," Marilla laughed. Then turning serious, she said, "But they always seem so friendly to you, Bess, and glad to see you."

"Hogwash," grunted Bessie. "They're friendly because we came from England where mother was a lady's maid and father was a gardener on Squire Ernst's estate in Westcombe there in Somerset. That doesn't mean that we have aristocratic blue blood flowing through our veins, but by some strange twist, Nettie has drawn her own conclusions, and she considers that somehow we have elevated social status. Besides, Nettie has a crush on Henry." Bessie rolled her eyes.

"What does Henry think of Nettie?" Marilla wondered.

"Humph!" was Bessie's resounding immediate response. "You know boys! I'd say that he's sometimes amused by her, but he's not impressed by her at all. He says she'll get her come-uppance some day."

I'm glad, thought Marilla. *I wouldn't want Henry to admire a girl like that.*

The group was back with the grownups by now, and Maureen waved a cheery goodbye. "See ya' later," she called.

"I like her. She's pleasant and cute," Cinda said.

Bessie nodded. "That she is, and she definitely has a mind of her own as well."

The town band began to play some lively music, and everyone sang patriotic songs and clapped. The weather had cooperated. There was not a cloud in the sky nor the chance of a shower to dampen the spirits of the citizens who took pride in their freedom.

But this year the celebration was somewhat somber. Everyone there knew that their beloved country was at that moment engaged in a fierce struggle. Word had come through the train station telegraph that a fierce battle had just ended in Gettysburg, Pennsylvania, and the North had won an important victory.

That was good news, for several families had loved ones in the Union Army. Nowadays whenever the men were together, their conversation automatically turned to the War of the Rebellion—even at a picnic. Marilla knew that a few years before some of the Southern states had withdrawn from the United States and formed their own government. Then Confederate soldiers—those were the

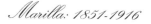

Southern soldiers—had attacked Fort Sumter in South Carolina. That was the start of the Civil War.

At first the war had seemed too far from Wisconsin to affect Marilla or her family. But then her own Uncle Stephen—her father's brother—had enlisted. Five months later Uncle Oscar, Mother's brother, also enlisted. Now suddenly the war seemed very close. Uncle Stephen came home about a year later with injuries from the terrible, bloody battle in Antietam, Maryland.

The family knew it was likely he'd eventually lose the sight in his wounded eye, and Marilla felt sad when she'd see him squint slightly. He'd always had such a sparkle in his laughing blue eyes. But otherwise he'd apparently recovered completely, and his sight did not seem to be too badly damaged, at least for the time being.

To bring the war even closer to home and even more devastating, her young Uncle Charlie—dear, curly-haired, fun-loving Charlie Turner had died after only four months of service. At that, the war grew very, very real to Marilla. She mourned with her family that a terrible price had been paid by Uncle Charlie and the men who died with him to help save Kentucky for the Union. No more would any of them hear Uncle Charlie's beautiful Irish tenor voice, or his telling jokes while his eyes danced with delight. Everyone who knew Charlie Turner cherished their memories of him.

Marilla's young heart stood still when she thought about all the killing and fighting. She was downright scared. Having her uncles serving their country was commendable, she admitted to herself, but somehow she could not shake the dread—an overwhelming dread—when she thought about her own father ever having to go to war.

Men killing men! It's worse than killing hogs! Dear God, please don't let Papa go to war. If he does, the sun need not rise again, nor the rivers flow, nor the birds sing. Forgive me for being selfish, but I am so frightened just to think of this awful conflict—the bloodshed. Please give me strength.

He just can't go. I won't let him, Marilla vowed in her heart, but she knew there'd be no stopping him if he decided to do so. Just thinking sent chills up and down her spine. So there she sat, the sun shining on her head, chilled at the thought of her father leaving, never to return.

Timothy Kelly and John Turner had long, serious discussions about the war whenever they got together. She'd heard them talking more than once. "Our country's in terrible trouble," she heard Father say to Mr. Kelly as they sat at the picnic table that Independence Day. "President Lincoln is a brave man, but it's an uphill struggle. I'm afraid it will take most of us to save the Union, and end this scourge of slavery." Father's voice was as serious as Marilla had ever heard.

She was glad when the Kellys began to gather up their belongings. Everyone else packed up, too, and soon they were all in their wagons, headed for home. The horses' shadows were long in the slanting sunlight. It was time to go. There were chores to be done.

Marilla wrapped her arms around her little sister's slender figure and cuddled her as they slowly rode toward home. The day had been exciting, and Annie Laurie leaned against Marilla, willing to rest from all the activity.

As the three wagons rolled along together, Mother suggested that everyone sing.

"How about 'When Johnny Comes Marching Home'?" Father suggested. "That's a good one." So Mother set the pitch and they all rousingly sang:

> "When Johnny comes marching home again,
> Hurrah! Hurrah!
> We'll give him a hearty welcome then,
> Hurrah! Hurrah!
> The men will cheer and the boys will shout,
> The ladies they will all turn out,
> And we'll all feel gay,
> When Johnny comes marching home.

Everyone joined in—the Parfitts in the first wagon and the Kellys in the last—until they were almost shouting at the last line of the song. Joe stood up in the moving wagon, raising and waving his hands to show them he was directing their chorus. But the wagon hit a rut, and Joe tottered, then clumsily lost his balance, and sat down in an unexpected hurry. Everyone had a good laugh at that. Not to be undone, Joe scrambled to his feet, doffed his straw hat, and nodded at his "choir," grinning from ear to ear.

"That boy has shot up like a beanstalk lately," Father said to no one in particular.

THREE

Fun and Fears

Summer slipped by sooner than the children wanted it to. The farm work and the gardening took up lots of time. Everyone worked hard—harder than they did in the winter, if that were possible. Yes, there were more times of wading and having fun, but children were expected to do their share of work, and work they did. Only if they finished their work early, did anyone have time to sit and relax. In the hot, late afternoons, Marilla and Annie Laurie would sit in the shade on the porch with their parents, and Barkley, and some of the cats. Often Mother and Marilla snapped beans or shelled peas as they rested.

Marilla had named one of the kittens Purrsia. "I'm sure he's a musician. Listen to him sing," she laughed. "His chest rumbles when he purrs."

"He likes to sing, just like you do." Annie Laurie held him gently on her shoulder and ruffled his soft fur.

"You have such a nice voice, Rilla," she said in her best grown-up way. "When we sing together in church I always hear your lovely alto. Mama says you have a good ear, too." She turned as her mother opened the front door. "You know that Mama is the best musician any-

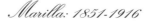

where, and she says your voice harmonizes well." Annie Laurie looked pleased.

Mother sat down on a porch chair, a large bowl over-flowing with green beans in her lap. "Yes, Marilla has a voice that blends. It isn't harsh nor does it stand out. It's soft and very pretty and never off key." She smiled at her older daughter.

"Thanks, Mama," Marilla said. Singing on key came easy to her, and harmonizing was fun. "I love to sing. It's just that I'm not a soloist. I'll leave that to you."

"The Eddys were a very musical family, and so were the Turners," Mother told them as if she'd never mentioned it before. "One of the things that attracted me to your father was that he appreciated music. When I heard him say that music was food for his soul, I knew he was the man I wanted to marry." Mother winked, and the girls laughed. They both enjoyed hearing their parents refer to their courting days.

"Papa surely does like to sing, and he has a good voice," Marilla said. "But all the Turner men sing well. It's always been fun listening to them harmonizing when we get together—at least we had fun before this miserable war interrupted our happy days."

Annie Laurie clasped her sister's hand. She did not completely understand the war, but she knew it was a dreadful thing. Anything that made her sister look so sad must be a terrible thing indeed.

"At least we have Papa here with us." Annie Laurie tried to be of comfort.

Marilla's face clouded. "But my heart aches when I think the day may come when he'll leave us to join the fighting."

Mother looked across the yard where Barkley sniffed at the base of a tree. "Now there, my girls, let's not fret and fume over something that hasn't happened yet," she said stoutly. "God will give us strength for every trial that comes our way. He's given us that promise." Mother was a pillar and a mainstay for her daughters, and her calm, steady temperament helped them take courage.

"Whatever would we do without you, Mama?" Marilla asked.

"Tell you what," Mother said. "Spread this clean tea towel on your lap and take a mess of these beans. With your help, we'll have them snapped in no time." She motioned to a bucket she'd set on the floor for the snapped beans. "Truth is, child, I don't know what I'd do without my daughters either."

John joined his family, whistling merrily. "How are my girls?" he asked, taking a chair next to his wife.

"I've an idea," he told them, mopping his neck with a kerchief. "Suppose we all climb in the wagon and go over to the Parfitts? It'll be light for some time yet, and we can easily get back before dark. I have a tool that James wants to use. The ride will do us good."

And tall John Turner lifted Annie Laurie over his shoulder like she was a bag of beans. She squealed and called for Marilla to save her. "I'm too big for you anymore, Papa. Help me, Rilla!"

Mother scrambled to get the bowlful of beans she was snapping into the kitchen. Marilla ran after her, tossing on the table the towel full of beans she'd been snapping. They were both laughing as they hurried to the wagon and Father helped them in.

The Parfitts were delighted to have company. While the grownups visited, the children played on the lawn with Duke, the Parfitt family dog. A border collie, Duke loved catching balls that the children threw into the air. He rarely missed a toss and even seemed to swagger as though he was proud of his ability.

Henry had taught him a lot of tricks, and Duke seemed to understand every word Henry said. The dog looked directly into Henry's eyes, tilting his head as he listened. "Wanna see his newest trick, Miss Annie?" Henry asked the little girl.

"Another one? A new one, really?"

"Wait till you see this one, Annie," chimed in Jim.

Henry called the dog to him and lovingly stroked its head. Then looking right into Duke's eyes, he said, "Duke, here comes the Lord Mayor. All rise."

Up went Duke on his haunches until Henry said, "Be seated."

Oh, how the children laughed, each one patting the dog's head and congratulating him. He wagged his tail wildly and barked as if to join in their laughter.

"I wonder what he'd do if you said Hail to the Queen. Would he bow his head in respect?" laughed Marilla.

"I'll train him to do that next," Henry promised her.

As twilight settled over the countryside and shadows lengthened, Father said, "Well, my ladies, it's time to go home. The crickets are calling us, and the lightning bugs will illuminate our way."

It had been a busy, happy, peaceful day with a wonderful ending. As the evening stars began to come out, Marilla thanked God for her nice family and for good neighbors. Then as her mind drifted to other things she wondered if the enemy soldiers could see the same stars that shone over Wisconsin.

FOUR

Good Dog Duke

Soon it was time for the annual cleaning bee at the Sweet Briar School. Just before school started, the parents came to clean, scrub, and polish until you could see your reflection in every desk and table, the blackboards and the walls were spotless, and the whole school ready for the new school year. The work was finished by mid- to late-afternoon. Then parents and students shared a potluck meal before they called it a day and went home. Every year the children looked forward to the festivities.

"It's like an extra fourth of July picnic," Jim Parfitt had told Cinda, and everyone, especially the students, agreed.

This school year brought extra excitement, for the new teacher had arrived from Boston. To the surprise of some and joy of all, Miss Eileen Donovan was right there at the work bee, washing blackboards, straightening the cupboard, and meeting the parents and their children. The Liberty community was very impressed with her. Not only was she well-mannered and kind, but she was charming, energetic, pleasant, and quite pretty. In fact, Marilla thought she was striking. It was the neatness of her dress with its hand-crocheted lace edging, as well the way she

carried herself and spoke to parents and students alike.

Dignified, that's what she is. I like her!

While the grown-ups and older students worked, Annie Laurie, Patty Ann Kelly, and Martha Latcher picked a bouquet of coneflowers, black-eyed Susan, and blazing star, and shyly brought it to Miss Donovan. She graciously accepted the flowers and searched until she found a jar. That gesture—displaying the flowers in water to keep them fresh—captured everyone's approval and respect. Even more important, it won the children's admiration as well.

When the work was finished, the men put planks across saw horses to make a long table under a shade tree. Two or three women spread tablecloths. Everyone was ready to eat by then. Bowls of potato salad and baked beans crowded cabbage slaw, loaves of bread, and cheese from the rich milk of Wisconsin cows. After working so long and hard they all had good appetites. At the end of the table were the desserts—pies, puddings, cakes, and tarts. Mother Turner's chocolate cream cake was always a favorite, and Annie Laurie took the credit for it this year.

"I made it all by myself. Well, almost all by myself. Rilla helped me," Annie Laurie acknowledged with a gracious, happy grin. Marilla smiled too, thinking of the help her 6-year-old sister had given. You could say that they'd both made the cake.

"Let me at it!" called Freddy Phelps, reaching across the table for a piece. His mother tapped his hand and told him to wait his turn.

"But it'll all be gone if Jimmy Parfitt has his way," Freddy teased, throwing a smile at Jim.

After eating their fill and cleaning up, at last everyone went home to their own chores, pleased that the day had been balmy and bright and that the school was "spanking clean," as Pastor Burlingame pronounced.

❦

On the first day of school, Marilla watched Miss Donovan's every move. All the children did. They took in her dark-blue ankle-length skirt and her crisp white blouse with a brooch at the neck. Patty Ann thought she was beautiful, the way wisps of hair curled around her cheeks, and the little girl unconsciously twisted strands of her own hair around a finger. The girls loved the mother-of-pearl comb she wore in her hair and whispered about it during the first recess.

The new teacher was pretty and gracious, but everyone wondered what she'd be like in the classroom. It didn't take long to find out, and they weren't disappointed. Miss Donovan's style of teaching and her own personality put the pupils at ease but kept them on their toes as well. Even the big boys complied with her request that the students always answer with, "Yes, ma'am" or "No, ma'am."

Miss Donovan was a kind but uncompromising disciplinarian, and the students sensed that by the end of the first day. She maintained order and allowed no tomfoolery. But at recess and after school, she was relaxed and

downright friendly. She was fun, Marilla decided, for from the very first day, school progressed well, even as teacher and students got used to each other.

"I'm going to establish a new tradition," Miss Donovan announced the first week.

A new tradition?

Cinda looked at Marilla with raised eyebrows. Marilla gave a slight shrug.

"Every week I am going to write a quotation on the blackboard," the teacher explained before anyone could ask questions. "And every day the whole school will repeat it together."

Marilla sat up a little straighter at that. This could be fun. In her imagination she already was . . . But Miss Donovan's voice drew her back from her daydream with the words ". . . end of the week students in grades five through eight will be required to write it from memory on their spelling test."

Squeaks from the back row drew the teacher's raised eyebrows. "The quotations will be both interesting and instructive," she added with a smile. "Learning them will increase and expand your vocabulary, and they will be good rules to live by."

The older boys groaned, but it was a good-natured groan, and even Miss Donovan rolled her eyes and laughed. "I should have expected that," she admitted.

"I'll talk about the principle of each of the quotes. That should help you remember them." She was so enthusiastic that the students began to think it could be fun. "I

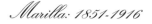

think you'll learn to enjoy the sayings," she promised. "Some will be humorous, but all will be worth your while to memorize. I call them my wisdom literature. I know you'll benefit by learning them.

"Our first quotation will be an excellent rule for all of us to follow. In fact, we might call it our Sweet Briar Motto. Even though they weren't yet good readers, from their place on the front row the first graders leaned forward so they wouldn't miss a word Miss Donovan wrote:

> "'Tis a lesson you should heed, Try, try again.
> If at first you don't succeed, Try, try again.
> Then your courage should appear
> For, if you will persevere
> You will conquer, never fear. Try, try again."

Miss Donovan turned with a bright smile. "Isn't that delightful?" she said. "I hope each of you will try to do your best this year." The children smiled, too—at their teacher and at each other.

"Tuck that into your memory and live by its inspiration. I'm sure that in just a short time, all of us, including the first graders, will be able to repeat this motto without any effort."

Marilla liked the motto. And she liked memorizing. She just knew she'd grow to love their new teacher.

Sometime later, Marilla had another pleasant surprise. Each of the older students was expected to memorize several dozen lines of poetry or prose from a reader or famous

book and deliver an oration before the class. While some would have felt terrified at the prospect, Marilla was thrilled. And when Miss Donovan promised to bring her own personal book of poems to school, the girl almost had to hold on to her desk to keep from jumping up with joy.

"You eighth-graders can look through the book first," she told that class, "since each of you will have a part on the year-end graduation program."

"What will we do?" Richard asked.

"Ah, that's to be determined," she said mysteriously. "I'll assign it to you when I see where your interests and abilities lie. I don't know you well—not yet, anyway. But as the year goes by I'll discover which of you are literary or musical, or in whatever way you excel." She looked so excited about it that the children couldn't help but be excited too.

Marilla was very pleased. This was just the type of challenge she liked. She couldn't wait to tell her mother about the assignment. "I love to do that sort of thing," she said. "It's easy for me, of course, but then maybe it's because I like words so much."

Mother sat down in the rocker and pointed to the chair next to her, which Marilla very willingly pulled up close.

"Yes, I know you like to read and memorize," Mother said. "I believe you learned to love the beauty of words from your grandmother Hannah Eddy. And I've always encouraged you to memorize things, as well."

"Spending time with Grandma was fun. She was full of

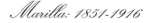

stories—about her own childhood and yours, Mama." Marilla's eyes twinkled as she looked at her mother.

"She never forgot a thing I did," laughed Mother, "especially the tricks your Uncle Oscar and I used to play on Ozro. My, that Ozro was a nuisance, though. He badgered me every chance he had. Sometimes I'd threaten him, but he'd laugh and tell me I'd have to catch him first. He was a pest and tease, but a dear pest and tease, nonetheless. I miss not having him close."

"I do too, Mama. 'Member how he'd jump from side to side over the saddle while Dobbin trotted along? He was a one-man circus."

"That boy took my breath away and your grandma's too!"

"I miss Wheatland sometimes." Marilla hugged her knees, thinking. "But it's so nice to have Cinda Kelly nearby. We like remembering the jolly times we had when we were little, and it's wonderful to have her back and with me in eighth grade."

"It *is* a comfort to reminisce with dear friends. You know, Julia and I go back a long way—all the way back to New York. We met on the first day of our wagon train trip to Wisconsin Territory." She paused, thinking. "Why, that was in 1843, 21 years ago!"

Marilla gave her a startled look. "That was a long time ago."

"You're right. Wisconsin had only been a U.S. Territory for nine years." She shook her head. "It was wild country. Not wild in the sense of frightening, but unsettled

country. When I think of our moving into the log cabin! I was so excited. We finally had a real house again."

"Well, I'm glad Wisconsin's a state now." Marilla looked out the window at the setting sun. The fall leaves glowed like fire in its rays. "But it would have been kind of fun to live back there in the olden days."

Mother laughed at that. "Olden days, indeed," she teased. "And what will your children be saying about your school days?"

"I'll tell them that I loved to memorize, and that they should too," the girl firmly declared. "I remember when Grandma Hannah gave me my Bible," she added, her voice gentle. It was before we moved here to Liberty, and she told me, 'Now you take care and see to it that you fill that little head of yours with knowledge, Rilla, my girl. God didn't give you such a bright mind for it to go to waste.'" Marilla tried to imitate her grandma's voice. "I remember that she told me to learn Psalm 91 just as you did, Mama, when you were my age.

"Then she gave me such a big bear hug, I thought I'd never be able to catch my breath again. She was a good hugger."

Mother smiled. "A good hugger, indeed!"

"Oh!" Marilla said, remembering what she'd wanted to tell her mother. "Miss Donovan said that I might want to learn a poem by Henry Wadsworth Longfellow. He's her favorite author. I think it would be fun to learn one of his poems."

Mother nodded, listening to her joyful daughter.

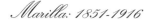

Shadows had darkened the room as they'd talked, so she'd gotten up and lit candles for light. Annie Laurie had slipped into the room, sitting down on the floor next to her mother's chair. Suddenly she piped up, "All the sayings and proverbs Miss Donovan reads to us make us feel important. She says that it's good to learn the words wise people have written in the past."

Mother placed her hand on her daughter's head and stroked her hair. "And you have done well, Annie Laurie," she said. "I am very pleased."

"So am I," said Father who'd just come through the door. "Miss Donovan is quite the teacher. She's not like any other teacher I've known. Learn all you can from her, girls."

Annie Laurie jumped up to give him a hug. "Right after lunch today, at story time, Miss Donovan read us part of Longfellow's new poem about Paul Revere's ride. She'll finish tomorrow. It was exciting. Everyone was so quiet that no one even wiggled."

Marilla agreed. "You could have heard a pin drop. Even the big boys behaved. 'Course the big boys are beginning to understand that they'd better behave. They like her, I think, although Erik and Richard thought she was a bit too strict at first. But she can be a lot of fun, too.

"She has a friend back at the library in Boston who subscribes to the *Atlantic Monthly*," Marilla continued. "It's a magazine that prints stories and things that have just been released. Well, this friend sends them on to Miss Donovan, so we get to hear some of these great pieces of literature even before they appear in books."

Both Mother and Father were impressed. "The day we met her I said to myself that we had hired a very special teacher," Mother told them. "And I was right!"

"Before I forget," Marilla said, "I've got to tell you what Wally said today."

Mother chuckled. "Knowing Wally Zimmerman, I suppose it was funny."

"Well, this week we have to memorize a quotation by Alexander Pope. He was born in 1688. Imagine! Anyway, it goes like this:

> "'Words are like leaves;
>   and where they most abound,
>   Much fruit of sense beneath
>   is rarely found.'

"Wally didn't need to have Miss Donovan explain the meaning of the statement. He turned his head to me immediately and said under his breath, 'Eulalie Cameron.' Of course, we giggled, and Miss Donovan tapped her desk. But it was very funny."

"Really now, Marilla. Be careful."

"But, Mama, Eulalie's well known for her incessant, rambling jabber. Erik calls it drivel, and Richard calls it poppycock."

"I do understand," Mother said, laughter in her eyes. "You'll be surprised that even your mother knows a quotation by Pope."

"Really?" Annie Laurie asked in disbelief.

"It's an old one, but I'm sure you've heard it said many times. It's 'Be not the first by whom the new are tried, Nor yet the last to lay the old aside.'"

"Yep, I've heard that one, but I didn't know the pope said it," Annie Laurie exclaimed, much to the delight of her parents and sister.

"Not *the* Vatican Pope, honey. Alexander Pope, the writer," Father explained, and Annie Laurie laughed too.

FIVE

Wisdom Literature

During October, Marilla's mother learned the good news that her own brother Oscar had been discharged and returned home. However, he was very sick. Marilla's young heart froze.

Oh, God in heaven, please help Uncle Oscar get well soon, she prayed fervently.

Despite the Union victory at Gettysburg several months before, the war continued. Each week the New London newspaper printed the latest news. The Union now controlled the Mississippi River, and that was hurting the Confederates. But one way or another, every month hundreds of soldiers on both sides of the war still died in battle.

When she told Cinda the good but also bad news about Uncle Oscar, Cinda was distressed as well.

"Oh, no. I'm so sorry, Rilla." She was almost in tears. "My Uncle Shane Kelly tried to enlist, but he was turned down because of his limp. Father was quite relieved in a way 'cause he said that Uncle Shane would have had a hard time walking or marching."

The girls were talking quietly by themselves as the rest of the school children played during the lunch break.

Cinda squeezed Marilla's hand. "It will be over soon," she said. "My father says that—"

Just then Miss Donovan rang a small bell. Everyone stopped their play and ran to the wooden stoop in front of the door. The two girlfriends, still holding hands, hurried to join them. "Please remember my uncle in your prayers, Cinda," Marilla whispered, and in that moment she thought her heart might break.

Cinda gave her a warm hug and together they stood in silence, looking up at a wedge of wild geese that flew honking high overhead in the clear, blue sky.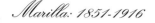

SIX

A Chinese Proverb

 The days came and went. They became shorter and cooler. It was dark when the students got up, and dark when some went outside to do their chores, but hardly any missed a day of school. Their studies were demanding, but not overwhelming. To Marilla, learning was enjoyment, not a task to dread. The more she learned, the more she wanted to learn, and she looked forward to her next assignments.

At recess, the youngsters ran off their energy. The fastest young girl runners were Annie Laurie and Maggie Phelps.

"Your legs must be part antelope," Cinda declared to the two of them after watching them run around the school yard and out into the road. "You ought to race with each other and see who could win,"

"I'm game." Maggie nodded vigorously, and Annie Laurie excitedly agreed.

"But if I win, Maggie, here's the deal. My old set of jacks needs a new ball. I saw a small red ball last week in Hill's general store." Annie Laurie was determined to make the race worthwhile.

Maggie said, "OK, but if I win, I'd like some of your famous chocolate cream cake. Is it a deal?"

It was agreed, and the goal they would run to. The two girls stood side by side. Erik held up his handkerchief and shouted, "On your mark. Get set. GO!" And he dropped the handkerchief with a flourish.

In the first seconds Maggie leaped out in front, but Annie Laurie's legs pumped like pistons, and then they were side by side. Their classmates jumped and cheered with excitement as the girls ran for dear life. Cinda, and Richard Latcher waited at the finish point and as the girls neared, it seemed they were neck and neck.

Later the watchers explained to Miss Donovan that the racers had been even—that is, until both girls reached out to touch the designated tree. In that instant a strange accident happened. Annie Laurie apparently twisted her ankle, and running at top speed, she fell sideways, bumping into Maggie. That threw Maggie forward, and she hit her head on the tree trunk. The race abruptly ended. Annie Laurie lay on the ground crying as she clutched her leg. Maggie was completely silent— perhaps knocked out for several seconds—but then began groaning and holding her hand to her head.

Cinda and Richard called for Miss Donovan. She came running.

Holding Annie Laurie in one arm, she gently stroked Maggie's hair from her forehead. "Get some water from the well," she instructed.

"Yes, Ma'am!" Richard snapped, and raced off. Marilla tried to comfort her sister, and Freddy Phelps held his sister's hands and looked worried. Richard returned soon

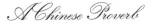

and both girls had a sip of water and tried to sit up.

"Easy, easy, Annie Laurie," said Marilla. "Can you move your leg at all?"

She could wiggle her toes, but she winced when she did it. It was her ankle that hurt the most, and it was beginning to swell. So Miss Donovan wrapped a cold wet cloth around it and gently pressed a cold handkerchief on Maggie's bump.

"It looks like an egg already, Maggie. You're just a little early for Easter." Richard tried to be light-hearted, but he did look concerned. Maggie smiled weakly.

Miss Donovan asked Erik and Richard to find some long sticks, as straight as possible. She placed the sticks on either side of Annie Laurie's leg and then bound it with a scarf as well as she could. The Kellys lived nearby, so Cinda ran home, returning with a wagon driven by her brother Ethan. Maggie and Annie Laurie were lifted into the wagon, and both "victims" (as Erik called them) were taken home.

"Off with you now, Ethan," said Erik, "and don't spare the horses!" Miss Donovan chuckled as she walked with Erik back into the schoolhouse.

Freddy looked grumpily at Marilla who'd stood watching them drive away. "All this wouldn't have happened if your sister hadn't pushed my sister. Annie Laurie just thinks she's smart!"

"She does not, Freddy, and you know it." Miralla felt her face get hot. "It was an accident. You heard what Richard and Cinda said. They saw it happen."

"Cinda's your best friend, and Richard would side with you. Maggie can run faster than Annie Laurie, and your sister didn't want to lose. That's it in a nutshell." And Freddy pushed Marilla aside as he stomped through the schoolhouse door.

Miss Donovan waited until he was in his seat then quietly asked, "What's the fuss?"

"Those Turner girls try to rule the roost around here, that's all." Freddy looked defiant. "Just wait till I tell my folks about this. Annie Laurie wanted to win so badly that she pushed my sister out of her way."

"Freddy Phelps, I'm surprised at you," the teacher said. "I'd like to talk to you after school."

Freddy turned his head and sulked. "Yes, ma'am."

The next morning the girls were back in school, none the worse for their accidents. "Well, that race was a tie, I'd say," Richard diplomatically announced.

"No, it wasn't," Annie Laurie said. "Maggie really won. She touched the tree first."

Everyone roared in laughter, looking at the blue knot on Maggie's forehead.

"Annie Laurie really would have touched the tree first if she hadn't fallen. Her arms are longer than mine," Maggie said seriously. "And I have her prize in my lunch box." Triumphantly, she handed the red ball to Annie Laurie.

"Hooray for Maggie!" someone shouted.

With a hesitant but gracious smile, Annie Laurie accepted the ball. Then she announced that she would bring a whole cake as soon as she could, and that everyone could have a sliver.

"But Maggie will have the largest piece," Annie Laurie grinned. Then it was her turn to hear the praise of her classmates.

"Three cheers for Annie Laurie!" they called.

"I told Freddy what happened—that it was an accident. Annie Laurie fell down. She didn't push me," said Maggie.

"I'm sorry, everyone." Freddy looked embarrassed. "Guess I just let my temper get the best of me."

Miss Donovan patted his shoulder. "It takes a courageous gentleman to admit he was wrong, Freddy. I'm proud of you. This reminds me of a Chinese proverb:

"'If you are patient in a moment of anger,
    You will escape a hundred days of sorrow.'

"Doesn't that make good sense? I'll put that on the schedule for us to memorize next week," she said.

Richard reached out and shook Freddy's hand while the several students looked on with smiles.

"I commend you girls for your generosity toward each other," Miss Donovan said. "All's well that ends well."

Everyone was glad that this problem had been happily solved.

SEVEN

Sweet Briar Christmas

As winter settled with snow and cold winds, Mother was grateful that her girls did not have far to travel to get to school. When the days were calm and the temperature not too low, Marilla and Annie Laurie enjoyed walking there. Other times their father or James Parfitt took the children of both families in a wagon. Either way they were bundled up from head to toe.

They didn't mind the cold weather. It was just part of life in Wisconsin. And besides, with snow came sledding, and soon the long cold days froze the lakes so they could go ice skating. But this winter brought something new to Sweet Briar School. Miss Donovan arranged to have their school join the school that had just begun in Northport in presenting a Christmas program. "It will be held in our school building because it's larger than theirs," Marilla excitedly told her mother one afternoon. "Miss Holden—she teaches at Northport School—feels that this is a good opportunity to let people know about their school *and* to boost interest in education. You know," she added seriously, "some people don't even send their children to school above the lower grades, and some youngsters don't even want to go!"

Mother nodded. She was counting the strokes as she beat cake batter, so didn't reply. She didn't want to lose count. Marilla understood. She chatted on, thinking out loud about certain families who didn't value education and what might be done about it. "I do think that a really good program by the students could change their minds," she concluded, "if they'd come and see it."

After church the next Sunday Miss Donovan asked Mother if she would play the piano for the Christmas carol sing during the upcoming program.

Mother was flattered. "I'm happy to do so," she said. "Music and I are friends."

Miss Donovan smiled at that answer, looking into Ann Turner's eyes. "From every corner of the larger New London community I've learned that you enjoy a prominent reputation. No one seems to doubt that you are the finest musician around." Miss Donovan reached for Ann's hand and shook it. "I do believe you are a celebrity!"

"No more than you, Miss Donovan," Mother told her. "You have won the love of my daughters and, I believe, of every child in your classroom and their parents as well."

❧❧❧

Afternoons, once school was out for the day, the children stayed by to practice the songs they'd sing for the Christmas program. A boy from Northport had been chosen to read the story of Jesus' birth from the book of Luke, and there'd be a live nativity scene with the children playing the roles of Mary, Joseph, the shepherds, and the wise men. Someone had suggested that the scene include a cow and sheep, but that was still under discussion. A Northport girl was to play a tune on her violin, and a choir made up of students from both schools would sing carols.

Richard accepted the assignment of reading "Paul Revere's Ride." It was a favorite of the students, and they never tired of hearing it over and over.

"It's quite a long piece, Richard, so I won't ask you to memorize it. But you read aloud exceptionally well," Miss Donovan told him.

Richard shrugged his shoulders and smiled. "I'll do my best."

"I'm sure you will." Miss Donovan gave him a friendly pat on the back.

Then she asked Freddy Phelps and Wally Zimmerman to sing a duet. "You both seem to love music," she told them with a smile.

They looked at each other, shrugged their shoulders, grinned, and agreed. When there was classroom singing, these boys enjoyed it immensely. It wasn't that they sang so loudly, but they were enthusiastic, and they had fun singing zestfully.

Marilla was asked if she would recite "The Night Before Christmas," by Clement Moore. "I'm sure you won't have trouble learning it," the teacher said.

Marilla's eyes sparkled. "I know it already!"

After school Marilla spoke to Miss Donovan alone. "Couldn't Cinda and I recite the Christmas poem together? I don't mean say it together, just take turns."

"What you mean is that you would recite it 'responsively,'" the teacher explained. "Perhaps every four lines or so. Let me work on it this evening, and I'll divide the poem so that you'll alternately recite each section. Maybe joining your voices together on certain lines." Surprisingly, she half-twirled in a little dance. "It's a *fine* idea, Marilla. This is one thing I love about teaching. My students always surprise me. Do you think Cinda will be interested?"

"Oh, I think so. Will you ask her."

"That I will, the first thing tomorrow morning."

Sure enough, Cinda accepted the assignment, although being a new student, she felt a little hesitant. "You'll do well, Cinda. Don't worry," Miss Donovan encouraged as she talked with the two friends during recess. "Now girls, since neither of you will have too many lines to learn, it will be much more impressive if you repeat the poem from memory."

"Oh, yes!" they agreed.

Eagerly looking forward to the program, Marilla and Cinda reviewed their poem forward and backward, until they could say it in their sleep. The other students were busy too. Miss Donovan had them rehearse their carols everyday, helping them sing clearly and teaching them how to use expression, even in song.

It was during one afternoon when the students were practicing the carols that Marilla got the idea to write a school song. She felt thrilled at the first thought of it, then let down. Poetry came easy to her, but she was no composer of tunes. Still, the idea wouldn't leave. She mulled the problem over in her mind for a full day before she went to her mother and told her that she'd had a wild idea to write a school song.

"Why not write new words to music that the children are familiar with?"

She was puzzled. "Like what, Mama?"

Mother closed her eyes, thinking. "Oh, maybe, 'Flow Gently Sweet Afton,'" she said, then frowned. "No. You need something less somber and dignified. Try 'Yankee Doodle.' It's a simple tune, and can be sung with vigor."

"Mama, you're a genius! You know that? I'll do it. I'm just going to do it." And off Marilla went, humming the familiar tune to herself.

❧

It was snowing lightly the evening of the Christmas program, but there was little or no wind. Mrs. Iversen and Mrs. Allen from the Northport community had beautifully decorated the school. They'd placed a red candle on a stand by the piano and lovely pine-branch swags at each window complete with big shiny, red bows. Pine fragrance filled the room.

As they waited for the program to begin, Cinda remarked to her fellow eighth-graders, "We're the oldest students here."

Erik straightened his tie with a flourish. "Doesn't that make us rather important?"

"You fellas look handsome tonight," Marilla said, looking them up and down. "And Richard, you've finally combed your hair!"

Through narrowed eyes, Richard pretended to look daggers at Marilla. His hair was a source of pride for him, and he always wore it neatly combed—the part as straight as an arrow.

"Well, thanks a lot, Marilla Sasparilla," he retorted with a teasing grin. "You're just jealous."

He'd given Marilla that double-rhyming name a long time before.

"That I am, Richard! Jealous," she laughed. "How I envy your wavy hair. Mine doesn't know what a curl is. The only wave it has is when one hair stands up and waves at another one."

"Well, I must say that you and Cinda look pretty dandy in your matching dresses," Erik told the girls. He was first and always a gentleman. "Did your mothers get together on the project? You're dressed like twins."

"My mother loves to sew," Cinda explained, "so she made both dresses. Marilla and I like Scottish tartan plaids. The only difference is that Rilla's is red and mine is blue. But they're the same pattern."

Both girls felt grown-up and glamorous. The long-sleeved dresses were trimmed with velvet and lace, and tiny pearl buttons embellished the high necklines.

"Are you nervous?" Erik asked them.

They both admitted that they were.

"I am, too," he confessed. "I've never prayed before such a large gathering." He was to offer the opening prayer.

"But you have a way with words, Erik," Marilla encouraged. "You'll be a preacher or a professor someday."

Erik grinned, raised his chin, and snapped his heels together.

"You're also a moderately miserable entertainer—lest you get the big head."

"And you, Marilla Gorilla, are a mediocre she-lion with a vicious tongue, but no teeth."

Cinda and Richard laughed but stayed out of the fray. They couldn't compete with Erik and Marilla when it came to the use of words, especially barbed one. They'd heard their two classmates go at it enough times to know there was just no way to win.

Richard nodded toward the two. "Right now, silence is golden for us, Cinda. I don't even attempt any rebuttals with those two."

Erik laughed at that. "Rilla and I don't even care who wins," he told Richard. "We just like to see who can come up with the most disagreeable, disgusting, and distasteful taunts."

Before Marilla could reply, Miss Donovan began lining up the students, starting with the lower grades. Still Marilla managed to whisper to Erik, "I can just see you behind a huge desk or some podium, expounding some theory or philosophizing"—she paused and dropped her voice even lower—"*when you're 45 with a bald head and spectacles.*"

"Funny," Erik murmured behind his hand. "I was just thinking the same about you."

Then it was all eyes ahead, all students watching their teacher for her next instruction. The program was about to begin.

The schoolroom was filled to capacity. Extra benches and chairs had been brought in, and yet some folks had to stand at the back. Marilla took a deep breath. At the front of the room she saw her mother at the piano. Then the first notes of "O Come All Ye Faithful" rang from the keys. One hand motioning time to the music, Miss Donovan nodded. Little ones first, the students marched down the makeshift aisle and took the seats reserved for them at the front of the room.

Miss Holden welcomed the parents and friends then asked everyone to stand. Erik stepped forward and presented the beautifully-worded prayer he had composed himself. As he took his seat, Marilla smiled brightly at him and mouthed the words, "Well done." He gave her a slight nod followed by an impish wink.

Trudy, the little girl who played "Silent Night" on her violin, got a bit mixed up, but found her place and finished successfully. She was only 7 years old, and everyone was pleased to enthusiastically clap for her. She blushed and curtsied sweetly, her curls bobbing as she bounced back to her seat.

Miss Donovan then introduced Richard. "I have asked one of our eighth-grade boys to present a work by Henry Wadsworth Longfellow. It's entitled "Paul Revere's Ride," and if you have not already heard it," she said, speaking slowly and clearly, "you are in for a thrill. This work will fill your soul with patriotism, and I think it will inspire you." She paused and looked over the room. Though every seat was taken, and people were standing in the back, more than one family was incomplete—their father or brother, uncle or cousin many miles away, fighting on soil that few there would ever see.

Miss Donovan continued, "At this point in our country's history our days are filled with anxiety. But I feel you will take heart when you hear of the bravery of our early American citizens in their fight for freedom."

Richard stood and read slowly, clearly, and with expression. His words easily held everyone's attention.

"'One if by land, and two if by sea;
And I on the opposite shore will be . . .'"

Richard knew how to read with feeling.

"'But mostly he watched with eager search,
The belfry tower of the Old North Church . . .'"

At times, Richard almost whispered, and the audience leaned forward so they wouldn't miss a word.

My he's gotten tall, Marilla thought. She glanced toward Cinda who was smiling her approval at Richard. *I think she's sweet on him!* Marilla inwardly grinned to herself.

Hearty applause exploded when Richard finished. He bowed, just as Miss Donovan had instructed. Next the combined group of students sang two carols. Then it was time for Marilla and Cinda's vocal duet. Marilla had thought she might be nervous, standing before a room filled with people, but she wasn't. Miss Donovan had explained that stage fright was real, but they didn't need to be afraid of it. "Don't look at the ceiling or down at your feet," she'd told all the students during practice. "Your audience is in front of you. Try to look at them or slightly over their heads toward the back of the room."

So the girls had practiced that, and remembered it when they stood up to speak. Book in hand, Miss Donovan stood off to the side, ready to prompt them if needed. But neither girl forgot her lines.

The audience followed along with the familiar words, smiling as they relived the imaginary visit of Saint Nicholas. Too soon the girls concluded with the familiar words, "'Merry Christmas to all, And to all a good night!'"

After the applause, Cinda and Marilla held hands and bowed, just as they'd practiced—discreetly nodding their approval to each other as they sat down.

Annie Laurie could hardly stay in her seat, she was so proud of her sister. She swung her legs back and forth with such energy that she almost slid off her chair.

There was a slight pause as Miss Holden and Miss Donovan helped the children involved in the nativity scene find their places. Then, Davy, a Northport boy, read the passage from the Gospel of Luke. He had practiced it over and over, and he read flawlessly.

As Davy read, the students playing Mary, Joseph, the shepherds, and the Wise Men stood or bowed or knelt as the Nativity script dictated. But one of the Wise Men dropped the gift he was holding—a small, brightly painted box—and quickly leaned down to retrieve it. In doing so

he bumped a shepherd boy who tottered a bit, before re-
gaining his balance. "Mary" sneezed loudly, but politely
covered her mouth. Still her face turned red under her
blue shawl, and she gave a quick look at "Joseph," who
raised his eyebrows and rolled his eyes in embarrassment.

Marilla saw Annie Laurie grin with amusement at
Patty Ann and Martha. The girls controlled themselves,
but it was obvious they wanted to laugh. The audience, of
course, was indulgent with pride for the children. No one
was critical. Rather, they delighted in the meaning and
beauty of the scene while appreciating the children's roles.

To close the program, the children from both schools
lined up in three rows to sing "Joy to the World." After
the first verse, Mother played a short bridge of music
while Freddy and Wally stepped forward and smoothly
sang the second verse as a duet. Their boy soprano voices
rang clear as a bell. Marilla noticed both Mrs. Phelps and
Mrs. Zimmerman touching their hankies to their eyes,
and then she saw the Widow Dexter do the same. Then
Miss Holden turned and led the entire congregation in
singing the last verse together with all the students.

Pastor Burlingame pronounced the benediction.

Though the program was over, folks seemed loath to
leave. They clustered in little groups, talking about how
well the children had performed. Many came up to shake
hands with the students and to congratulate the teachers
on a job well done.

The older girls of Sweet Briar School thought their
teacher had never looked prettier. The deep red of her

Christmas dress set off her dark hair, and her eyes sparkled with joy. She almost looked like an angel.

"We've never had such a nice program," declared the Widow Dexter to Miss Donovan as she shook the teacher's hand. Behind her stood her tall son, Darby, who also took Miss Donovan's hand. "It was an impressive program," he said quietly. "Thank you."

Marilla's eyes turned to her mother who was standing nearby. As their eyes met, Marilla knew that her mother knew what she was thinking.

What is Darby up to?

Never had she known Darby to say much to any adult. Now here he was making a short but cordial statement to the new teacher with seeming confidence and ease.

Gradually the audience thinned as folks bundled up their younger children and went out to their wagons for the trip home down the snow-packed road.

The eighth-graders didn't want the evening to end. "You spoke well, ladies," Henry said with a wide smile at Cinda and Marilla. "I was proud of you both." Then turning to Annie Laurie who stood next to her sister, he bowed low and officially shook her hand. "And as for you, young lady, Queen Victoria herself would say you look smashingly gorgeous tonight."

Annie Laurie blushed but grinned back at Henry.

"He's right," agreed young Jim Parfitt. "You look like a princess. All you'd need is a crown on your curls."

Annie Laurie looked straight at Jim and coyly said, "I'm glad you noticed, Jimmie."

Bessie put her arm on her young brother's shoulder. "That was a nice compliment, Jim. I didn't know you had it in you."

"You must have just kissed the Blarney Stone," Cinda teased. "Right, Jim?"

The poor boy blushed and looked sheepish.

"Never mind, that was gentlemanly of you, little brother. I'm proud of you." Henry gave him a pat on the back.

"You and Cinda have such pretty dresses for the holidays, and they'll be nice all winter long." With admiration, Bessie touched the velvet trim on Marilla's dress. "Well, I think Father and Mother are waiting for us."

"Bye, Rilla," Henry said with a wink.

Bessie playfully grabbed his arm and pulled him along. "He'd stand here all night just looking at you, Rilla. See you soon. You, too Cinda."

EIGHT

Papa Goes to War

Then it happened—tragedy on a cold winter morning. Hardly two weeks after Christmas, Marilla and her family sorrowfully bid Father a sad farewell at the train station. "Goodbye, Papa! Come back soon!" the girls called as the train carried him away.

John Turner was on his way to Madison to be mustered in to join the Union forces in the Civil War. Where he would go after that, no one knew.

Marilla felt as if she were dreaming. The events of the last weeks overwhelmed her while she recalled each detail.

As the war had dragged on, Father became determined to help President Lincoln. After much discussion, Timothy Kelly—Cinda's father—volunteered with him. Uncle Stephen, Father's brother, reenlisted too. Marilla had wondered if Uncle Stephen would be accepted, having been wounded in battle when he was in the army before. But apparently, Army physicians had agreed that he was fit to serve. *Maybe*, Marilla reasoned, *with the war going on for so long, they need more soldiers*.

It seemed especially bad to them that Father left in the winter. The days were short, the nights long and dark. Chores were even harder in the wintertime. Their neigh-

bors, James Parfitt and his sons, took on the responsibility of assisting Mother during her husband's absence. They had promised John Turner that they'd see to it that things went smoothly on the farm while he was gone. It was their way of helping the Union win the war.

As for the Kelly family, Ethan and Jared pledged to their father that together, all the Kellys could do the farm work. Other neighborhood men who were unable to serve, vowed to help out whenever needed.

It hadn't been an easy decision for Father. Marilla knew that. Cinda knew it too—for that matter—about *her* father. Even before Christmas the girls had confided in each other, for both had overheard their parents discussing the war. The men were torn between love for their families and the growing responsibility they felt for their country. With the war going into its fourth year, and with so many men being killed in battle, Father could not justify his remaining on the farm when so many men had given their lives for their country. And yet, he could not imagine leaving his wife and two daughters to care for the farm.

Father and Mr. Turner had talked for hours. James Parfitt often joined them. Finally, the decision was made. There were tears in Father's eyes as he told his wife and daughters.

It wasn't for nothing that as a child Marilla's mother, Ann, had said goodbye to her Grandpa and traveled weeks in a wagon train to the untamed Wisconsin Territory. Now she drew on the strength of her pioneer roots. "Remember, John," she said, "during the War for

Independence women stood behind their men. They planted and harvested the crops. They helped each other, and they prevailed."

She held up one hand when he started to speak. "I've even heard how the women on Nantucket Island competently ran their farms and their local communities while their men were away on whaling expeditions for a year or more at a time. So, my dear John, don't you worry about us. We'll do all right."

Wind-blown sleet peppered the outside walls of their home, but the fireplace gave a little warmth and candles added a soft glow. Even though she felt overwhelmed with sadness, Marilla's heart warmed at her mother's words and her father's reply.

"I knew I could count on you, Ann. You are the backbone of my life." And he had wrapped his wife in his arms as they both wept.

"I am compelled to go, my dear. So pray for me, and for all the men who are determined to see the end of this ordeal."

The days had flown by in a flurry of preparation. Now the time was at hand, and Marilla was waving goodbye to her wonderful father. He seemed more precious to her in that moment than he ever had before. The tears she'd been holding back ran down her cheeks and splashed on her coat. How long would he be gone? When would they hear from him? She was lonesome for him already.

Marilla glanced down at Annie Laurie who'd pressed

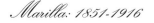

close to her side. Snowflakes lightly danced on her red woolen cap and stuck to her eyelashes. Then the engine gave a loud *whoosh*, and steam billowed from the smokestack and pistons. The train chugged forward, gaining momentum, and the girls sadly but bravely waved until it was completely out of sight.

Their mother stood behind them, an arm around each girl's shoulders, hugging them tightly. "We will pray everyday for God to watch over him," Mother said, still watching the cloud of steam that drifted in the distance. Then drying her own tears, she gently led the girls to the wagon and let the horses take them home.

The countryside was covered with a blanket of white, yet Marilla saw no beauty in the world. The wind was sharp, and she was grateful for the shelter of the trees as the horses jogged through the woods. No one spoke. There was nothing more to say.

That night in their bed, Annie snuggled next to Marilla and tightly grasped her hand. "Papa said for me to be good and brave," she whispered tremulously, "but I'm awfully scared he'll get hurt." So Marilla held her close, and together they cried themselves to sleep.

Will this nightmare never end? was Marilla's last thought as she drifted into a troubled slumber. She was so afraid that she might never see her father, Mr. Kelly, or her uncles ever again.

Most of the children at school had fathers, brothers, or uncles fighting to save the Union. Every morning, the children sang the song "My Country, 'Tis of Thee."

Deep in her heart, Marilla cherished the beginning words of the anthem:

> "My country, 'tis of thee,
>   Sweet land of Liberty,
> Of thee I sing."

That's why Papa is out there somewhere, so that freedom can ring from every mountainside.

One gloomy, gray day not too long after Father left, Marilla asked Miss Donovan if she could just stay in during recess. Sensing that the girl needed some time to herself, the teacher said yes.

"Would you like to help me hang the pictures our lower grades have drawn, or would you like to talk?" Miss Donovan asked.

That was the only opening she needed. Her eyes filling with tears Marilla asked shakily, "Do you think this war will change my father?"

Miss Donovan took Marilla's chin in her hand, and looking directly into her tearful eyes said, "If he is a good man, yes. He'd have to change." Then drawing Marilla into her arms, she just held her. The young girl's slim body shook as she sobbed.

"You will find, Marilla, that as time passes, you will feel better. Right now, it's so close to when your father's left on that train that the sadness of merely waving goodbye to him is still unbearable. But your burden will lighten."

Marilla tried to speak, but the words wouldn't come. It

was so confusing. The Southerners—no the Confederate Army—were so far away. What did they have to do with Wisconsin anyway? Some said that they were fighting for the right to be their own boss. But that didn't make sense. Why did they want to pull out of the United States? Others said the South was fighting for the right to own slaves, that they would lose their plantations without them. But what about the *slaves?* Both Father and Cinda's father said that no one should own another *person.* Father was fighting to save the Union and free the slaves.

It was just too much to comprehend.

Comforted there in her teacher's arms, gradually Marilla stopped crying. She pulled back a bit and accepted the hanky Miss Donovan put in her hand. "Oh, thank you," she said, drying her tears. "I try to be strong for Mama's sake. But today was just too much, I guess. I'm OK now." She managed a brave if shaky smile.

Marilla took Miss Donovan's suggestion that she get some fresh air before recess was over, so she grabbed her coat and scarf and went out to find Cinda. She wasn't surprised that her friend leaned against a tree, a faraway look in her eyes. Now the girls were bound even closer by a new and special bond. Each knew the other's heartache and loneliness. As the days turned into weeks, sometimes they just held hands at recess as they fought to hold back their tears.

Dexter Darby Wakes Up

Mother knew that keeping busy was the best way to ease their loneliness while Father was gone, so she encouraged her girls to study their school lessons faithfully. Then there was the farm. Although it was not large, the work was demanding. Early mornings were dark and very cold, but still the cows and horses had to cared for before they went to school. Paths had to be shoveled and kept clear in the deep snow. The fireplace, ever hungry, demanded log after log after log. Thankfully, the Parfitt men kept check on the woodpile and made certain the Turner women had good wood to burn.

Mother labored vigorously and bravely, getting up and tending the fire in early morning before awakening the girls. Often the scent of hot soup and biscuits greeted them when they got home from school. For their part, the girls followed her example. Wisconsin winters are bitter, and it wasn't easy wading through deep snow to get to the barn or the well, but they did it and tried not to complain. The livestock had to have food and water, just as they did.

During that long winter, many were the times Marilla saw the lanterns of Henry and one of his brothers when she looked out the window in the predawn darkness. Caps

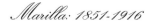

on their heads, scarves wound around their necks, she'd see them shoveling a path from the house to the barn. Then they'd break through the layer of ice in the water trough, so they could water the livestock.

On quiet nights when the work was done, the girls would knit or sew while Mother told them stories. Marilla loved to hear about the amazing night when the stars seemed to fall from the sky, and both girls took great pleasure in hearing their mother relive how she fell in love with and married their Father.

In her girlhood dreams, Marilla wondered whom she might marry one day. Theirs wasn't a large community, but she couldn't help but notice the young men. Girls usually married while still in their teens, and both Cinda and Marilla knew they could be married in four or five years. As girls will do, sometimes they talked about the different fellows, checking them off on their fingers and listing their good qualities.

No matter how much they giggled about one young man or another, Henry Parfitt always seemed special to Marilla. She felt sure he liked her, too, though she didn't know if it could be more than big-brother friendship. But her heart skipped a beat when he'd wave a friendly greeting. He was easy to talk to, and he told her interesting and fascinating tales describing how he'd met and befriended the Indians who had a camp upriver. He often visited them, and had learned a little of their language. Marilla didn't know anyone else near her age who'd done that.

"The Indians are awfully good trappers," Henry explained. They'd taught him their ways of hunting and trapping, and he knew every tree along their trails and trap lines. "Somehow, though, I just can't hunt and kill deer," Henry told her. "Their eyes always look so mournful when I go to haul off their bodies. It's a look of betrayal that I can't get out of my mind's eye, so I just won't do it. But there's no finer feeling than coming home with four or five muskrat pelts." His face brightened, recalling the feeling. "I've learned how to skin off the hides and stretch them on boards. Pelts can be changed into a handful of silver dollars, you know!"

Yes, Marilla thought, *Henry is the nicest and the smartest boy I know.*

Marilla and Annie Laurie were often included in the Parfitt children's sleigh rides and other fun times. Henry and his brothers even made it fun to come to the Turner farm to check that the family didn't need anything. And Marilla loved going to their house. While Henry played "Turkey in the Straw" on his father's fiddle, the young folks clapped their hands, tapped their toes, and now and then even jumped up and twirled. Somehow despite her loneliness for Father, Marilla's heart felt lighter when she visited with this good, kind English family.

One cold, snowy day as Mother and the girls worked in the kitchen, she paused and said, "Hark, what's that I hear?" The girls stopped talking and listened. Nothing. But when Marilla ran to the window she saw Henry with an axe.

Mother was right behind her. "Come on in, Henry,"

she called from the doorway.

"Thanks, but no thanks. Father asked me to stop by and check your supply of wood."

"How nice! Well, come in when you're finished and have a mug of hot chocolate with us."

Whistling, Henry strode toward the back of the house. Marilla grabbed her coat, cap, and mittens and joined him at the woodpile. "We appreciate your help so much." Her breath hung like a cloud of vapor in the air.

Henry stopped chopping for a moment and said with a grin, "It just gives me a chance to see you and your blue eyes."

"Flattery will get you nowhere, sir."

"Well, at least I gave it a try!" he said with big smile. "Anyway, I'd like you to be the first to know this, Rilla. Mr. Schubert—one of the lumber barons in New London—well, he's asked if I could work part-time in the agency office. The men there feel that because I'm so well acquainted with the land and forests around here, I'd be good help to them—filing records and researching documents."

"Oh! Wow!" Marilla gasped. "A really truly job."

"It's a great opportunity," Henry said, picking up another log. "My parents have agreed that I can do it, even though just part time. Truth is, I'm rather pleased that Mr. Schubert is interested in me."

Marilla looked at him with new eyes. "Why, Henry!" she exclaimed. "That's a compliment—truly! Mr. Schubert is well-known and respected. May I tell Mama and Annie Laurie?"

He nodded. "Yeah, that's OK. It's soon to be known anyway. But I just wanted to tell you myself." He balanced the log and raised his axe. "Bessie teases me dreadfully. She says I'm going to be nothing but a 'flunky' in the office, but I can tell she's pleased, too."

Marilla laughed. "She's just your pesky little sister."

One day Miss Donovan asked her students if they'd mind staying in during recess. "It's frightfully cold," she pointed out, "and I've received a new magazine from my friend in Boston."

They didn't have to be told that it was cold outside. It was so bad that heat from the schoolhouse stove had raised the inside temperature by a just few degrees. The children agreed, so the teacher led them in standing up, stretching their arms above their heads, and walking around the room four times. It was fun, and they were laughing and relaxed by the time they went back to their desks.

Miss Donovan explained that the poem she would read was written by John Greenleaf Whittier after he'd received word from a friend in Washington, D.C., about a 97-year-old woman who lived in Frederick, Maryland.

As she read, the children learned how an elderly woman, Dame Barbara Frietchie, showed her patriotism. The poem told of something that happened in Maryland when the Confederate army of Northern Virginia marched into the town of Frederick, General Thomas

"Stonewall" Jackson leading the way. People flying the American flag quickly took them down when they heard that enemy troops were coming. But Barbara Frietchie refused to follow the example of her neighbors, and bravely hung the Stars and Stripes from her upstairs window. When the Confederate soldiers parading down her street saw the flag, an officer gave two short commands: "Halt!" and then, "Fire!" The flag was damaged by the bullet, but Barbara Frietchie still refused to take it down. In fact, it's said that from her attic window where she'd hung the flag, she called a reprimand to the soldiers still standing on the street below her home.

The rhythm of Whittier's poem grabbed Marilla's attention. She leaned forward to listen as Miss Donovan read the first lines:

> " 'Up from the meadows rich with corn,
>   Clear in the cool September morn,
>   The clustered spires of Frederick stand
>   Green-walled by the hills of Maryland.' "

The rhythm and rhyme of the story poem carried the students along, forever preserving the memory and words of Barbara Frietchie:

> " 'Shoot if you must this old gray head,
>   But spare your country's flag, she said.' "

After Miss Donovan read the last words the room was

quiet, then an excited, inspired Patty Ann declared without even raising her hand, "You know, Annie Laurie Turner, come next fourth of July, I'm gonna dress up like old Barbara Frietchie and march in the parade carrying a flag!"

Catching the spirit, Jim Parfitt announced, "I'll be right there with you beating a drum."

"Hurray!" others called, and Miss Donovan just laughed.

"Hurray, indeed!" she agreed. "It was a brave thing that old lady did."

The children's interest and attention had been captivated. It was a poem they always remembered.

❧❀❧

The winter blizzards were giving way to spring snowfalls. Marilla still missed her father, but Miss Donovan had been right. It had gotten easier. Still nights were the hardest. Their home felt so empty without him, and sometimes she almost forgot that he wasn't there. She'd run toward the house with some bit of news, then stop short. With a deep breath and a prayer for Father's safety—wherever he was—she'd slowly open the door.

Yet spring was on the way. The wind had lost the worst of its bite, and the sky was a different color. She couldn't help but feel happier.

As the school year slipped by, Miss Donovan began preparing her students for the eighth-grade graduation ceremony. Of course, Erik, Marilla, Cinda, and Richard were the stars. "Our school has never had a graduation ceremony before," Richard told the teacher. "This is a first."

"Probably because the eighth-grade class wasn't big enough—only one or two students," was Erik's response.

"But now we're four. And, besides, we're worth it!" Marilla laughed.

"Well, I'm the teacher now, and I say we'll have a ceremony." Miss Donovan nodded her head with a smile.

The four students joined their teacher in planning the program, sometimes staying after school hours to discuss their roles in the event. It was fun, and that they had a part in the planning made them feel even more grown-up.

More and more often, Darby Dexter dropped by after school to talk with Miss Donovan, to bring her something, or to take her on some errand in town. The eighth-graders smugly smiled at each other whenever Darby came around.

He was, of course, no stranger to any of them. Growing up, they'd often gone on hayrides or sleigh rides pulled by Darby's magnificent black mare. The horse had four white feet so, of course, was named Boots! Whenever they saw Darby ride by they'd wave and shout, "Hey, Darby! Hey Boots!" Darby was always quiet, but he'd wave back and grin.

And now? It seemed a bit of a surprise to the eighth-graders and to everyone else, that Darby Dexter, the only child of the Widow Dexter, was suddenly debonair and charming. In fact, Cinda and Marilla thought that it was almost like seeing a frog turn into a handsome prince!

Darby was a nice young man. He'd always been kind to the youngsters and friendly when they waved, but he was withdrawn around adults. And everyone thought him the typical dyed-in-the-wool bachelor.

But then Miss Eileen Donovan had come to town, and gradually Darby became a different fellow. He shocked everyone by the change—from the somewhat unsocial, withdrawn farm boy to a dashing, eligible gentleman. He even took notice of his clothes, and started dressing up. He really was quite handsome. More and more the young couple had been seen riding around in his new buggy. Everyone thought they made a splendid pair.

Long before, knowing that Darby was not at ease with people his own age, Marilla had asked her mother why it was that he didn't have a wife. "He's a nice enough fellow, though he doesn't talk much," Marilla said. "Even shy little Martha Latcher likes him and easily talks to him when she can't seem to find courage enough to speak to other folks."

Mother had explained that when he was a boy, Darby had been dragged by a horse in a miserable but not serious accident. His face was scraped and his arm and leg broken. The doctor stitched up a cut in his jaw just in front of his ear, and it healed quickly. It left a scar.

Darby was embarrassed by the scar. And it must have hurt him badly, Mother explained, when rude children teased him by calling him "scar face." Being naturally quiet like his father, it was easy for Darby to withdraw from people. Girls his age seemed to ignore him, and he was willing to let it go at that. Through the years the scar lost its redness and faded into nothingness. No one even noticed it anymore.

And so Darby had faded into the wallpaper, so to speak, and no one gave him much thought.

His parents, Carlyle and Olive Dexter, were some of the earliest settlers in the community. "Lyle" had worked hard to provide well for his wife and son. Everything he did flourished. He succeeded in buying extra property, and his farms prospered, and Darby capably assisted his father in every way.

Lyle and Olive had befriended the Turners when they moved to the community. A quiet, unassuming man, Lyle was loved by all, and everyone mourned his death just two years past.

Olive Dexter, on the other hand, was not known to be delicate or tactful. She was forthright to the point of being blunt. "Now, Ollie," Lyle would say when she would get on her high horse.

But, as Marilla often heard her mother claim, "Olive Dexter's heart is large as 10 hearts, and she just has to be taken with a grain of salt. She does not yet possess the 'ornament of a meek and quiet spirit,' but she is a wonderful friend, nonetheless."

❧

"Darby came to pick up Miss Donovan after school again today," reported Annie Laurie to her mother as she rushed through the door one afternoon.

"Well," answered Mother, "I'm not surprised that Darby has awakened to the world around him. It's about time." She looked beyond Annie Laurie, at Marilla, with an I-told-you-so expression. Marilla understood. ❀

TEN

Graduation Day

 Gradually, winter melted away for good. Spring had been slow in coming, but it definitely was on its way. "I can smell it in the air," Mother told her daughters one sunny morning, "and I'm so glad. I pray daily that your father is warm and well-fed wherever he may be."

"Can you believe it, Mama? I'll be graduating soon. It hardly seems possible." Marilla stood at the stove stirring a pot of oats. If she turned slightly she could see pale green shoots brightening the winter-brown grass. "This year really is speeding along. I can't believe it. Sometimes I pinch myself to make sure I'm not dreaming." She stopped, swallowing hard. "Oh, if only Papa could be here to see me receive my diploma."

"I know. I know," Mama said with a sigh. "But even though he's not here, he's as proud as can be of you."

She brushed off the table then stepped to the cabinet for three bowls. "Do you realize, my dear, almost-grown-up daughter, that you now will be eligible to teach school?" Ann's eyes widened with pride as she looked at Marilla.

"But I don't know very much, Mama."

"You know more than children who have never gone

to school. Therein lies the difference."

Marilla could not help but feel both elated and fortunate. She knew that even in some areas of the United States there were no schools, and she thought about other countries where girls were not allowed the privilege of an education under any circumstances. She could not imagine life without school. She loved learning far too much.

One day Miss Donovan asked if she might like to memorize Longfellow's "A Psalm of Life" to give at the graduation ceremony. "I think it would be most appropriate," she'd said in her formal way.

"Oh, yes. Yes!" Marilla was thrilled at the thought, but the teacher had even more to say.

"And I might just as well tell you now, Marilla, that it appears you'll be finishing the school year with the highest grade point average. You'll be the valedictorian."

"You mean I'm ahead of Erik?" Marilla could hardly believe it.

"It's true. You and Erik have been running neck to neck, but this last grading period you've pulled ahead."

Marilla was overwhelmed. She didn't want to gloat, but she felt extremely proud. Erik had always been keen competition, and she admired his brightness. To beat him in the race for grades was a compliment.

Boosted by this happy news, she decided to tell her teacher that she'd composed a verse that could easily be sung to the familiar tune "Yankee Doodle." "It could be our school song," she added hopefully.

At that, Marilla slipped a sheet of paper out of a textbook and handed it to Miss Donovan. When she read it, her face broke into a wide smile. "This is wonderful, Marilla. Just wonderful. Aren't you clever! Why, I'm going to have the children start practicing it tomorrow. They will love it!"

She hugged Marilla, paused to look at her at arm's length, then hugged her again.

Just as she'd predicted, the children were elated with the idea of a school song, and were overjoyed that it was so easy to sing. In a short time, every student knew the words, for they sang it every morning.

With courage and determination Marilla forged ahead with her studies. The days were getting milder and it was often hard to keep her mind on history or math. But she was so close to being the top student. She didn't dare allow herself the luxury of slacking in her schoolwork.

The only thing that did take her attention from her books was the obvious fact that Miss Donovan and Darby Dexter were serious in their friendship. "They're courting," Cinda and Marilla whispered to each other, and imagined their pretty teacher a guest at the Widow Dexter's table or on a picnic with the dashing Darby Dexter.

So it came as no surprise when the couple announced their engagement. Miss Donovan told her students as soon as it was decided. "Mr. Darby and I will be married the end of June," she announced. Everyone clapped, the

older girls looking at each other with satisfied expressions. Miss Donovan's eyes shone and her cheeks were pink as she quite properly said, "Thank you." She was very pleased that her students gave her their support.

And now it was April. For Marilla's and Cinda's birthdays Mother gave a small party. Mrs. Kelly and Patty Ann came too. It wasn't a big celebration, but it was nice to relax with friends. Not having their fathers there rather dampened the girls' delight, but the chocolate cream cake Annie had helped her mother make was eaten with pleasure.

Marilla gave Cinda a small sewing box with a quilted top. She put a new needle and a spool of thread in it, too—Cinda's favorite color, sunshine yellow. Bessie gave Cinda two new crochet hooks and a large spool of pretty lavender crochet thread.

Cinda gave Marilla a small book of poetry that Miss Donovan had recommended, and Bessie brought her a tin of assorted chocolates. Marilla promptly passed it around so they could all have a piece, then she quickly replaced the lid and put the box behind her back. The group laughed at her comical gesture, and politely no one asked for more.

While Patty Ann and Annie Laurie played dolls, the others sat in the front room. The conversation ranged from the upcoming graduation to the latest news from the battlefield to speculation of the teacher's wedding. *It was a lovely day*, Marilla thought that evening as she readied herself for bed. *Even without Father, it was a happy birthday.*

❧

The last day of school seemed to sneak up on the students like a thief in the night. No one could believe the school year was truly over. But graduation day was special. The cloud-covered sky threatened rain, but by some miracle the rain did not come.

Marilla wore a new spring dress that her mother had arranged for Mrs. Kelly to make, a pretty blue sprinkled with small flowers. It suited her perfectly and matched her lovely eyes. The rounded neckline and puffed sleeves trimmed with white eyelet lace were femininely attractive. Slipping into the dress on graduation day, Marilla swirled round and round, watching herself in Mother's bedroom mirror.

"I've never had such a beautiful dress, Mama. Thank you so much." She stopped, pensive. "I wish Papa could see me," she said, giving her mother a grateful hug.

"We'll remember *everything* so we can tell Papa," Mother reassured her.

Annie Laurie gave a little bounce from her perch on her parents' bed. "You look as lovely as a bride, Rilla," she complimented her big sister. "Did you pinch your cheeks? They're pretty and pink."

Mother stroked her younger daughter's head. "I let Marilla use a bit of my rouge, just for the occasion," she explained. "She deserves the little touch of elegance for the good work she's done."

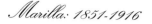

The graduation program was not long, but it was excellent. Miss Donovan had a certain ability to make things run smoothly and with decorum. Her own personal composure and dignity added to the magic of the event. The school house was filled with proud parents and guests—among them, of course, was Darby Dexter.

After all the students stood and sang "My Country 'Tis of Thee," Pastor Burlingame offered a heartfelt prayer—remembering the men of their community who were bravely serving their country and who could not be in attendance. He prayed, too, for the graduates and for their future plans.

To start the program, Erik, the class president, read a history of the school that he'd researched and prepared. He named the families involved in founding Sweet Briar School and recalled its humble beginnings and early struggles.

The audience laughed as he told about the time John Turner had to rescue Clayton Phelps who'd accidentally gotten stuck in the chimney of the old log schoolhouse. He also humorously related how his mother, Mrs. Iversen, had met a skunk while clearing out the thicket behind the log-house school. And then, to add insult to injury, she acquired a bad case of poison ivy as well.

"Take it from me, her firstborn," he said solemnly, "she hasn't been the same since!"

Mr. Iversen briefly interrupted the laughter by nodding and vigorously confirming his son's statement, holding up his hand and saying, "It's true! It's true!"

Erik recited the names of former students and teacher, and he honored three of those students who had met untimely deaths—Clarence Dunlap who had drowned, Fannie Stewart who had died in childbirth, and Adam Stevens who had been killed in a logging accident.

It was sobering to remember how fragile and short life could be. Marilla pushed the thought away because her mind had flown to her father. "Dear God, please bless him today," she prayed, then drew her mind back to the program.

To close his remarks, Erik recited Sir Walter Scott's, "Love of Country."

> "Breathes there the man with soul so dead
> Who never to himself hath said:
> 'This is my own, my native land'?
> Whose heart hath ne'er within him burned
> As home his footsteps he hath turned
> From wandering on a foreign strand?"

He spoke with expression. His performance was flawless and polished. *He's getting as good at public speaking as Richard is,* Marilla thought, feeling very proud of him.

At the poem's first words the room had grown quiet. Even the small children stopped wiggling. And when Erik uttered the last beautiful word, the audience enthusiastically clapped. Everyone was proud of him, but even more, they were proud of their school. "Love of Country" was an appropriate selection, too, considering the state of the

Union and the war that was—at last—drawing to a close.

As Erik turned to take his seat, Miss Donovan rose, put a hand on his shoulder, and told the audience that the Iversens had decided to have Erik continue his education in New London. Everyone clapped again, for most students didn't go beyond the eighth grade.

Next Cinda and Richard Latcher read the class will. The graduates had worked together on it, and their teacher had given her approval. This was something new, and the audience listened with amusement as, one by one, items were bequeathed to their classmates.

When Richard said he was leaving his comb to Wally Zimmerman, the children howled with delight. Wally's hair was never in place. It was clean, and it was short, but it was always disheveled. But Wally was not to be undone. He stood, grinned, and gave a slight bow, smoothing his hair with dramatic flair.

The schoolroom filled with laughter, and Freddy Phelps playfully reached out and tugged at a tuft of Wally's hair.

Then the four graduates stood together. With well-chosen words, Richard spoke for all of them, thanking their parents for their love, encouragement, and support. Then from a vase of a dozen strikingly beautiful red roses on Miss Donovan's desk, each graduate drew a single flower and presented it to their mothers in a touching tribute.

Miss Donovan rose. "Last on our program we have another talented student, Marilla Turner, who will recite Henry Wadsworth Longfellow's poem entitled, 'A Psalm of Life.' This is one of his most memorable pieces of literature. Miss Donovan signaled for Marilla to stand.

"Marilla has finished at the head of her class. She has been a joy to teach. To see her grasp a principle, theory, or idea has been a source of great pleasure for me. I wish for her happiness and success as she journeys through life. Marilla, please." And Miss Donovan motioned the girl forward as she herself stepped aside.

"I am dedicating the recitation of this poem to my father, John Turner, who as you all know, is serving our President and our country somewhere in Kansas," Marilla said. Then after a poignant, silent pause, she raised her head and began:

> "Tell me not, in mournful number,
> Life is but an empty dream!—
> For the soul is dead that slumbers,
> And things are not what they seem.
>
> "Life is real! Life is earnest!
> And the grave is not its goal;
> Dust thou art, to dust returnest,
> Was not spoken of the soul. . . .
>
> "Lives of great men all remind us
> We can make our lives sublime.
> And, departing, leave behind us
> Footprints on the sands of time. . . ."

Once more the audience was riveted in rapt attention.

Many of the folks had not heard this work by Longfellow, and they were enjoying it to the fullest. Marilla continued her recitation and ended with the words:

> "Let us then be up and doing,
>   With a heart for any fate;
>   Still achieving, still pursuing,
>   Learn to labor and to wait."

Standing motionless for an eloquent moment, Marilla smiled politely at the audience, turned to Miss Donovan and nodded, then took her seat. The clapping that followed was like thunder. Someone in the back whistled.

Miss Donovan had Marilla stand again. "This talented girl has given a legacy to our school that none of us will forget. Not only has she left an excellent example for all students to follow, but she has used her many talents to cheer us, to brighten our days with merriment, and to revive us during these long days of desperate hope that all of us have endured, along with our beloved President Abraham Lincoln."

Looking out over the room, Marilla caught her mother's eye. She was looking up, her face shining, but her eyes were focused somewhere beyond the teacher. Marilla wondered if she was thinking about Papa, but Miss Donovan's voice brought her back to the present.

"One day in early spring Marilla approached me with the idea of a school song," she was saying. "She had composed the words and set them to a tune familiar to all of

us—'Yankee Doodle.' I was amazed—even amused—as I read the words. Now you may have already heard your children singing this song. They have loved practicing it. Now it will be officially performed for the first time—the new Sweet Briar School song."

She turned to her student. "Congratulations, and thank you, Marilla Turner!"

The teacher motioned for the students to stand and face the audience. They began singing without accompaniment as Miss Donovan directed.

"Our Sweet Briar School is great,
    We study and we learn here.
We strive to be good citizens,
    To do our best each school year.
We're Sweet Briar girls and boys,
    We're Sweet Briar scholars.
And we study hard to be
    as bright as silver dollars!

Everyone cheered at "bright as silver dollars," and some even joined in as the students sang it through a second time. Sitting tall in his chair, his eyes on the song's author, was Henry Parfitt.

The song ended. Miss Donovan waited for the elation to subside, then presented the graduation certificates to the four graduates.

The school year was officially over. Sweet Briar School had four new graduates.

Richard, acting on impulse, pulled another rose from the vase and handed it to the teacher. She smiled her thanks, and the audience softly murmured, "Awwww."

Then Miss Donovan continued, thanking her students and their parents for a wonderful, gratifying school year. "I believe I have learned as much as the children have," she said.

She paused, and the room paused with her. What was going to happen next? Cinda and Marilla nudged each other though their eyes looked straight ahead.

"And now I'm going to ask Darby Dexter to join me here in front."

"Oh, boy!" Richard's exclamation was but a whisper, but the graduates heard it.

Darby, dressed in his best church coat, shirt, and tie stepped forward and took Miss Donovan's hand with a smile. She nodded to him, and he said with pleasure and pride, "There will be a wedding in late June to which you are all invited. Miss Donovan has made me both proud and happy by accepting my proposal of marriage!"

He lifted Miss Donovan's hand and kissed it, then turned and winked at the children who clapped and grinned at each other. Marilla squeezed Cinda's hand. This was real romance. Romance up close! And she thought they were the most handsome couple she'd ever seen. Miss Donovan was positively radiant, and Dexter Darby had turned into a charming and handsome prince almost right before their eyes.

Then suddenly Pastor and Mrs. Burlingame stood by

the couple. Mrs. Burlingame held a bouquet of spring wildflowers such as violets, Dutchman's breeches, and wood geraniums, all nestled in delicate ferns. She gave it to Miss Donovan with a kiss on her cheek. The pastor cleared his throat. "This has been an exceptional school year for Sweet Briar," he began. "I have received compliments from all over the greater New London area. Miss Donovan's reputation has spread far and wide. Now I have the pleasure of telling you that the future Mrs. Dexter has agreed—with the wholehearted approval of the school board, as well as with Darby's complete support—to continue with us next year. Just how long she will stay remains to be seen, but we are delighted to have her with us."

Almost without thought, the school children stood and clapped loudly, grinning from ear to ear. The audience stood too, clapping their approval.

When the applause died down, Miss Donovan, herself, gave the benediction. Then the crowd milled around the schoolhouse, laughing, congratulating, and visiting. The children hooted and hollered as they ran outside. The school year was over!

Erik, Richard, Cinda, and Marilla stood together at the front of the room, thanking the people who came to congratulate them and to shake their hands.

When the graduates finally had a moment to themselves, Marilla turned to Erik. "It's just great that you're going on to high school, Erik. You will do well and go far, my dear old friend."

"Why don't you join me, Rilla? With your brain and mine, we could show up anyone who'd want to challenge us!"

"Thanks for the invitation and the kind words, but for now I'll stay home with Mother. At least until my father returns. We don't know when that will be, but we pray it will be soon."

Cinda locked arms with her classmate, pulling her close, and Richard shook their hands. With a glint in his eye he said, "My parents and you lovely young lassies may think of me as forward, but I'm going to kiss you both!"

"If you can, I can," said Erik with a determined, boastful look. So each girl got a peck on her cheek from the boys who were their cohorts all year.

With the crowd absorbed in groups of conversation, no one seemed to be noticing the graduates. No one, that is, except a young man named Henry who stepped up behind Marilla and said, "As long as congratulations are going 'round, here's mine." He kissed Marilla's other cheek, then shook her hand and held it warmly.

She gave him a big smile. He always made her feel good. "Thanks, Henry. I'm so glad you came."

Then Bessie was there, hugging Marilla and saying, "There'd have been no stopping him from being here. Did you hear him whistle? Mother almost fainted with embarrassment!"

"So that was you, Henry?" Marilla felt her face getting red, but she smiled proudly.

Turning to Cinda with a wink, Bessie said, "How

about that Darby? Wasn't he something?"

While the young people were absorbed in excitedly contributing their own particular viewpoints concerning the continuing saga of Darby's transformation, Henry took Marilla's elbow and drew her aside. Handing her a small box, he said, "This is my graduation gift for you."

She lifted the lid and saw a highly-polished gray stone which he explained was a Petosky stone. "I found it myself along the shore of Lake Michigan, and I polished it, too," he said. "Perhaps you can use it for a paperweight. It's not a rare stone, nor a precious one, but it is curious and distinctive. See the little fossil embedded in the stone? I had fun getting it ready for you." He finished with an almost self-conscious, flustered shrug, not typical of the confident Henry she knew.

She was thrilled. "How nice of you, Henry!" she exclaimed. "It's very attractive. I'll always cherish it, and value it more than its weight in gold because it came from you. Thanks."

He beamed. "Thanks to you, too, the sweetest girl in Wisconsin!"

She hugged that compliment to her heart. She and Henry were only friends, but he was the nicest boy she knew.

The evening was a huge success, and long remembered by all.

ELEVEN

The Wedding

 Marilla was excited. On the morning of the special occasion, she was up early.

What a wonderful day for Miss Donovan's wedding! she thought. *Guess I had better do my chores so I can be ready on time. Mama won't stand for being late, especially since she's the organist. Not that I want to be late either. I wouldn't miss a moment of this day!*

She quickly got busy and hurried with her work. When all was finished, she said, "Come, we'd better get ready, Annie Laurie." She led her sister to the kitchen where their mother had bath water heated and ready in the big, round tub.

Later Marilla helped Annie Laurie get dressed and fixed her hair—placing the white ribbons right where Annie wanted them. "How is it that you're so lucky to have wavy hair when mine is so pathetically straight— straight as string."

"But Mama says that your eyes are your shining glory. And your hair shines, too, 'cause you brush it faithfully every night." Annie looked at her sister with admiration. "Martha Latcher and I have secretly agreed that you're the prettiest girl in school."

"Am I now? 'Tis thankin' ye, I am. Faith, you'll be makin' me cry." Marilla tried to fake an Irish accent, but she knew she didn't sound as authentic as Cinda did.

She put on her own lovely blue graduation dress and a small straw hat with ribbon flowers. Mother wore her taffeta dress, a brooch that Father had given her, a small black straw hat, and a fleecy shawl that she'd knitted herself.

As they drove to the church in their wagon they met other folks headed the same direction, and everyone waved greetings. It was a very special day and all were enjoying the good weather and the happy occasion.

The church was beautifully decorated with several large bouquets of white lilacs, ribbons, and ferns. Mrs. Iversen had artistically worked her "magic" again. Her husband, too, had done his usual creative work by replacing the pulpit with an arbor arrayed with white flowers and ribbons. It was a lovely backdrop for the minister and the bride and groom.

The Turner girls quietly slipped into their regular front-row pew.

Then Mother began to play soft music on the small pump organ. She could get beautiful harmony out of the old instrument like no one else could.

Many times through the years Mother had reminded her daughters, "Every time I place my hands on the keys I remember how kind Mrs. Maguire taught me to play the piano back in Kenosha County where I grew up. 'Always use your talent to honor your Creator,' she'd say, and it was advice I'll never forget." The Maguires were in the same wagon train as Mother and her parents on the trip from New York to Wisconsin Territory.

It didn't take long for the church to fill. It was hard not to turn around every time they heard new footsteps or voices, but Marilla and Annie did their best, sneaking a peek behind them only now and then. Annie Laurie was so excited she could hardly sit still, and Marilla felt quietly happy. She even let herself dream of her own wedding . . . someday. And the future groom? She wouldn't let herself visualize him, but she did dream of walking down the aisle—or even of standing in the front room of their home—wearing a beautiful dress, a bouquet of flowers filling her arms.

Then James Parfitt stepped up near the organ with his violin. Mother lifted her hands from the keys, then gently dropped them and played a few soft notes. The violin joined in, and organ and violin accompanied Clayton Phelps who sang a solo. Marilla liked his rich voice. It was deep but soft, and he had a modest posture about him that she admired. He didn't seem to think he was better than anyone else, even though he had the best baritone voice in the whole community. It made hearing him all the more enjoyable.

The solo over, Mother pulled out all the stops and began pumping away at the pedals, playing the wedding march as loudly as the old organ would allow. The rafters seemed to shake.

Marilla tapped her fingers to the rhythm—*Here comes the bride, la la la la.* She softly hummed the familiar tune.

All eyes turned to see Miss Donovan. Now they could turn around and look!

She looks just beautiful! Beautiful. I hope I'll be that pretty when I get married some day, thought Marilla.

Annie Laurie's eyes were big as saucers. She was enthralled. Their parents had taught their daughters proper church decorum, and both girls understood that neither noise nor whispering was permissible in God's sanctuary. So Annie Laurie sat stock still, her eyes on the couple. Marilla was just as absorbed in the event as her sister.

There stood Darby, a young man Marilla had known for years. And beside him was the love of his life, Miss Eileen Donovan. After a short homily, Pastor Burlingame invited the couple to repeat their vows. They looked lovingly at each other as they said, "I do."

"I now pronounce you man and wife," the pastor intoned. When Darby leaned forward and gave Eileen a kiss Annie Laurie wiggled on the bench and reached for her sister's hand. Marilla gave her small hand a squeeze.

"I now present to you, Mr. and Mrs. Darby Dexter," said the pastor. Immediately Mother started the familiar recessional. The happy couple marched out of the church, the congregation right behind them. Darby lifted his new wife into a shiny buggy and they rode off in a shower of rice while the school children chanted, "There goes the bride! Take her for a ride!"

Then everyone scrambled to get into their own buggy or wagon to follow the couple to the Dexter home for a reception. Marilla and Annie Laurie had to wait until

Mother played the last note of the recessional before she joined them at their wagon. The girls were eager get to the party, and they weren't disappointed.

The house was filled with people, but the new Mr. and Mrs. Dexter were the center of attention. Even so, Annie Laurie was excited to see the raspberry drink and so many pies and cakes that they wouldn't all fit on the table.

Olive Dexter proved herself that afternoon. She was a perfect hostess—gracious to everyone. Her sister Violet was there with her, scurrying around doing much of the serving and organizing, giving instructions to the ladies who helped. Violet Tyler looked so much like her sister Olive that Marilla thought they could have been twins. Violet was agreeable and cordial, and for the first time that Marilla had ever noticed, Olive followed her younger sister's example. Violet had never married, but she certainly wasn't a "shrinking violet" by any means.

Marilla's mother had told her that many years before Violet had been engaged to a nice young man named Joshua Upton. There had been some misunderstanding between them, and the wedding was postponed. A year or so later they had been reconciled, but a month before the scheduled wedding Joshua was killed in a hunting accident. The broken-hearted Violet never fell in love again. After a period of mourning, she decided to take an active part in society. A capable and talented seamstress, she opened a little shop and kept herself busy.

She was admired by her many customers, and greatly loved by her community. Probably because she was not married, her parents had bequeathed their home to her at their deaths. It was a grand, spacious old house. Violet liked to entertain, and people enjoyed her pleasant afternoon teas and evening musical soirees. Word had spread that Olive Dexter would move in with her sister, leaving the Dexter home to Darby and Eileen. They had invited— no, almost demanded—that she stay in her own home. But Olive had said No. She wanted the new couple to have the house to themselves. "Eileen shouldn't always be looking over her shoulder, wondering if she's doing things the way I'd do them," she'd confided to friends.

Violet was in her element on this lovely afternoon. She pleased everyone by her gracious manner. Darby was his Aunt Violet's favorite, and she helped to make this day special for him and his pretty bride.

With tears in her eyes, Olive told Violet and Mother, "Lyle would be so proud of his son. I wish he were here."

༺❀༻

Marilla and her friends, Bessie, Cinda, and Maureen Murphy, strolled around talking, sampling the desserts, and simply enjoying the occasion. There was much to discuss—the latest style of the bride's new dress, the romance of her coming to teach and falling in love with such a nice man, and a few giggles about which of the four of them would be the first to marry. Quite by accident they overheard Eulalie Cameron peevishly say to Sadie Sawyer, "If I had known what a knock-out Darby Dexter would turn out to be, I sure would've set my cap for him long ago."

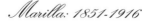

"I quite agree with you," replied Sadie. "When we were growing up who would ever have guessed that he'd become such a catch. It's too late now, but I sure wish I'd given that Eileen a little competition. I'm as good looking as she is," she said, coyly patting the curls on either side of her head, "even if I don't have her education."

"Oh, dearie, you know that it's the new face in town that men take a fancy to," Eulalie teased.

The two of them were known as flirtatious and superficial. Eulalie unabashedly carried herself a bit too brazenly, and Sadie, also, was known to display some coquettish behavior when she chose to. Put Eulalie and Sadie together, and they caught the eye of every male around, both the good and the bad.

Marilla and her friends slyly smiled at each other about those petty remarks, and continued to walk by. But when they were out of hearing, they laughed aloud.

Bessie was the first to react. "Doesn't it do your soul good to see those girls eat their hearts out? Last year they wouldn't even nod their heads in poor Darby's direction, and now look at them. Serves 'em right!"

"They seem to think a lot of themselves," Cinda said dryly.

"You've got that right," Maureen agreed. "Themselves, their dresses, their shoes, their hair—"

"Mother says that 'beauty is as beauty does,' and she means it," Bessie pronounced. "As for my brother Henry, bless his superior soul, he says that if he ever sees me acting like those two stuck-up girls, he'll disown me." She

spun around, laughing. "And 'speaking of the devil,' look who's here!" Bessie took Henry's arm as he and some friends joined the girls.

Each fellow had a piece of cake in his hands and was taking large bites with great relish. "What's so funny, girls? I can tell you're feeling smug about something." Henry smiled disarmingly.

"You wouldn't understand, big brother," Bessie laughingly told him. "Beside, this is girl talk."

They all laughed at that, but Henry countered with, "Try me."

So Bessie reported the conversation overheard from the two disappointed young ladies. Then the group had a good laugh together.

"Typical of those two." Erik nodded his head between bites.

"Sounds like sour grapes to me," said Ethan. "What is it with women anyway!"

Richard chuckled. "They've been bitten by the green-eyed monster."

Everyone agreed.

"Couldn't have said it better myself," laughed Bessie.

"H'mmm," was Henry's only reply, and Marilla could tell from the look on his face that he was considering what had been said. He generally tended to think before he spoke.

Then scratching his head and with a twinkle in his eye, he said, "Well, as I see it, Eulalie tries to be the belle of the ball at every wedding, even if she hasn't been the chosen bride."

"Hear, hear!" Maureen laughed.

"In my opinion, those two are flighty, shallow, and empty-headed. Decent fellows don't take that kind for wives," were Henry's last words.

Marilla looked at Henry with admiration. She had hoped he would see it that way. *I like him and I like what he said. Someday he'll make some girl proud to be his wife.*

The fellows walked on, and the girls went back for more raspberry drink.

Then the music began. Mr. Parfitt, with his fiddle, and Mr. Phelps, on the guitar, started playing lively tunes. Pastor Burlingame stood and suggested a grand march. He often called the directions on such occasions, and everyone enjoyed his creative ideas in giving intricate but amusing instructions.

Young and old lined up and began to tap their toes.

Henry offered Marilla his hand. Jim, Henry's young brother, playfully took Annie Laurie's hand and jumped in front of his brother. Annie Laurie looked over her shoulder with a smirk, and Henry gently pulled one of her curls, saying, "You think you're smart, don't cha?"

"Yes!" she giggled. It was so much fun to be included with her sister's friends.

Erik followed Henry's example and took Patty Ann's hand. Bessie stood with Ethan, Cinda with Richard, and Maureen and Jared lined up behind them.

They had a wonderful time, listening and minding the pastor's directions, winding in an out, circling here and there. It was confusing and exciting, this long line of

friends and family. Marilla's favorite step was when the line of partners faced each other, making a tunnel with their upraised arms and hands. Then the couple at the very end of line bent and snaked under the tunnel of arms, each next couple following the other in time with the music. At the end of the tunnel they took their place at the end of the line, their upraised hands extending the tunnel.

At last the fiddles, harmonicas, and other instruments stopped. The marchers dropped into chairs or leaned against a wall to catch their breath. There was time to visit some more until it was time to go home.

TWELVE

Sick, but Safe

 The farm work took the Turner's attention the rest of the summer. They worked from before dawn until dusk. Even with the help of the Parfitt's and other neighbors, there was almost more work than they could do. But the crops did get put in. They were cultivated, and finally harvested. With Papa gone, Marilla shouldered more and more responsibility. She couldn't help but see the weariness on her mother's face and quietly decided that she'd do whatever she could to make things easier for her.

In the fall, she often hitched up the wagon and took Annie Laurie to school. It was fun to see Miss Donovan, no, *Mrs. Dexter*. Now and then they talked about poetry or things going on in the community. Evenings, when needed, Marilla helped Annie Laurie with her classwork.

When word reached them that Uncle Ozro had enlisted, Mama sat down in a chair and buried her head in her hands. Marilla and Annie Laurie were dismayed. What should they say? What should they do?

Marilla felt as limp and helpless as a newborn kitten. She knew how her mother felt about her little brother Ozro. She knew how she, herself, felt about her spirited, animated, wild-riding uncle.

To her surprise, Marilla saw her mother's dry face turn to look out the window. "I have no more tears left," she said solemnly. "My heart is aching until I fear it will break. But this one thing I know—God understands our trials and sees each falling tear that is shed by the citizens of our community and country. I trust Him completely even though I do not understand His plan for me right now."

She held out her arms to her girls, and they fled to her, each embracing the other.

It's about time I bear and share Mama's work load. I've seen how weary and tired she looks at times.

Marilla longed for the day her father would come striding down the road, up their steps, and home. How she missed her beloved Papa. Just to have him around to talk to would be such a relief.

In any spare time she had, Marilla had started reading her Bible. It brought her both comfort and relief from the everyday cares of the world. The Bible became her treasure and delight, and she became an eager student of God's Word.

She was intrigued to read the Ten Commandments, and to see that God had set apart the seventh day of the week as Sabbath. She wondered about that, and as she continued her way through the Bible discovered that the Sabbath theme continued throughout the whole Book.

One Sunday when talking with Pastor Burlingame after church, she asked, "What about the seventh-day Sabbath, Pastor? How did it get changed to the first day of the week?"

His answer puzzled her. "Oh, my young sister Marilla, don't you let that bother you. We can honor and praise God any day of the week."

Somehow that statement and its implied assurance did not bring her peace of mind. In the days that followed she thought of it again and again. At last, in her young heart she promised herself, *If I ever find a church that keeps the seventh day holy, I'm going to join it.*

Occasionally, when Mother's shoulders seemed to especially sag, Marilla would give her a hug without saying a word. Mother would brush her hair from her forehead, straighten her shoulders, smile, and with determination move on. Marilla understood. Life just wasn't the same, but life must go on.

She is such a great woman and mother. Oh, how lonely she must be without Papa!

The war had ended in May, but Father hadn't come home. He still had more time to serve, and there was much to be done as the nation began the journey of healing the wounds of war. He was able to write more often now, and for a time after a letter arrived Mother would seem more hopeful and happy. Both Annie Laurie and Marilla noticed the difference.

"We must continue to take this one day at a time, girls," she reminded them as the summer leaves started to change color. "But one day soon, Papa will be home."

Marilla hugged her mother. "You'll always have us to count on, Mama. Never fear."

And then in mid-October Father arrived home. He

was sick, but he was safe. For his ability and bravery, Father had been promoted to Commissary Sergeant in Company L, 3rd Regiment, of the Wisconsin Cavalry there in Cow Creek, Kansas. They couldn't have been prouder of him!

How wonderful it was to see him sitting at the table or in his chair near the fireplace. Mother could hardly take her eyes off him, but then, neither could his daughters. He was thin and weak. His pale, drawn face reflected the scurvy and other illnesses he'd suffered during his tour of duty. Marilla looked at him with love, thinking, *Daisy's good milk and Mother's cooking will soon help that.* The family was overjoyed to have him and thanked God again and again.

Marilla's uncles, and Timothy Kelly had returned home too. The whole community rejoiced, and Pastor Burlingame announced that there'd be an early Thanksgiving community dinner held in the Sweet Briar School to celebrate the safe return of the men as well as to honor those who, sadly, would not be coming home. Eileen and Darby Dexter had extended the invitation.

༺✿༻

"You are our hero, Papa," Marilla proudly told him as they strolled arm in arm one unexpectedly warm fall day.

"War has many heroes, Marilla. You were a soldier's daughter who helped to keep the home fires burning while I was far away. So you see, you, too, were a hero." He stopped to catch his breath. "You were—and I think you still are—a very brave young hero."

Their footsteps crunched through the dried leaves blowing across the narrow lane. She leaned herself close to his side as they slowly walked along. Shuffling leaves with her feet, she was quiet and so was he—neither of them saying a word. She looked at the azure sky and took a deep breath.

Papa definitely wasn't the strong, healthy man he had been. Even now, she sensed a hesitancy in his step. Taking a sidelong glance at him, she felt sure he had stories to tell that he could not speak of yet. But he was alive! He was home.

Marilla's heart swelled with pride for her brave father, and she squeezed his hand. Then her eyes lifted to the blue, blue sky.

Thank you, God in heaven, for my many blessings, she prayed, *but especially right now for my father and for his safe return. Amen.*

The Rest of Marilla's Story

During the months that her father recuperated from his service in the army Marilla continued to energetically help her parents. There was a lot of work to do, but the Parfitt and Kelly boys were always on hand to pitch in with friendly assistance when needed. At school, too, the new Mrs. Dexter appreciated Marilla's help. Often when Marilla took Annie Laurie to school or picked her up afterward, she'd offer to do whatever task her former teacher needed. Marilla was creative, and had fun designing new material for the bulletin board and adding little decorative touches here and there. Gradually she became Mrs. Dexter's right-hand gal!

Mrs. Dexter resigned at the end of the next school year—for the best of reasons. By the time school started again Darby and Eileen Dexter welcomed a new family member. The school board began a hasty search for a new teacher and was pleased to find Rachel Cochran, a cousin of Eileen Dexter. After an interview, the board hired her on the spot. But until Miss Cochran could arrive from the East, Marilla filled in at the school. Delighted with the challenge and the chance to actually teach, she carried full responsibility for the students and the school for two weeks. The children took an immediate liking to the new "teacher" they'd known all their lives!

Cinda Kelly helped her mother establish Milady's Shoppe in town—a dressmaking and tailoring shop which became an almost overnight success. Julia Kelly was an excellent seamstress, and her daughter had her special talent, too. With Marilla on the farm and Cinda working at the dress shop, the girls didn't see each other as often as they wished. However, they visited whenever they could.

Maureen Murphy, a friend of both girls, frequently stopped by to see Cinda at Milady's Shoppe. As time passed, more and more Maureen's brother Pat stopped by to tip his hat to Cinda, too. When they managed to get together, Marilla and Cinda whispered about Pat and it was no surprise to Marilla when the couple announced their engagement. Nor was it unexpected when, at about the same time, Henry sought Marilla's hand in marriage. Both girls were blissfully and buoyantly happy. Only Nettie and Susanna seemed less than excited about both engagements!

Marilla and Henry married in 1868, when Marilla was 17 and Henry 21. Interestingly, four years later, Annie Laurie married Henry's younger brother, James. Bessie and Joseph had married earlier and all three families lived nearby in New London.

Henry tried farming when he and Marilla were first married, but he never liked it. He liked wandering the outdoors too much. At Marilla's suggestion they moved to town so they'd be close to the grade school. Marilla was anxious that her children would have no trouble getting an education, so neither Henry nor Marilla were disappointed at his decision to give up farming.

Henry knew the great woods of Wisconsin so well and was so accurate in all that he did that large lumber companies immediately asked him to work for them. His skills were needed to estimate how much timber could be cut and collected from a certain area. He traveled as far as Alabama and Louisiana in this job.

In later years Henry was smart and creative about finding work to help support his growing family. He owned and operated a boat, taking groups of people on picnics and other outings in the summertime. He even made ice cream! In 1894 the local newspaper wrote: "When you want a milk shake go to Henry Parfitt's near the south end of the bridge."

During the last part of his life Henry was constable of New London. His good dog Tip was always by his side.

And Marilla. She made a home for Henry and their 10 children. Jokes and laughter were as important as the hard work that it took to keep the home going. As her boys often stated, "There's never a dull moment at our house!" Marilla had considerable insight when it came to evaluating her children's different abilities, and did her best to encourage them to excel in whatever life work they chose.

You'll read more about Marilla in *Hannah's Girls: Grace*, which is Book 3 in this six-book series.

More About
Marilla's World

It might seem strange that Marilla didn't go on to high school, but most young people didn't in those days. Six to eight grades of schooling were considered a good education, and many young men and women taught after finishing all eight grades.

One Nation, East and West

At last, in 1869, the last spike was driven. Now the railroad ran across the entire United States. The settled East was finally linked to the "wild" West. The 3,000 miles between the East and West coasts could be traveled in only seven days.

Planting Trees

April 22, 1875: The first Arbor Day. This was the beginning of a campaign to get people to plant trees on the vast prairies of the Midwest. Within 12 years 600 million trees had been planted there.

Centennial Celebration

From January through December 1876, towns and states celebrated the one-hundredth birthday of the

United States. The biggest "party" of them all was held in Philadelphia where the Declaration of Independence had been signed 100 years before.

The Civil War

Every city, every town was touched in some way by the War Between the States. Families were literally divided, depending upon the state in which they lived. The long arm of the conflict reached all the way to Wisconsin, drawing its young men (and older) into its terrible battles.

Battle of Gettysburg

Seventy-five thousand Confederate soldiers had invaded the North. They were determined to win this battle and bring the war to an end. The fighting went on for three long days, and at last the weary Union soldiers defeated the Confederate.

Now nearly 150 years later people still remember this decisive battle. They visit the battlefield to honor the men of both sides who fought so hard for what each believed was right.

Battle of Perryville, Kentucky

Nearly 7,500 Union and Confederate soldiers died in this battle. In the months that followed hundreds of the sick and wounded which were staying in makeshift hospitals in almost every home and other buildings in the area, died every week. Charles Turner was one of them.

The Adventist Church: First, they started printing.

1850: In the summer of 1850 James White printed the first issue of a magazine he called *Advent Review*. In November this small magazine was combined with *Present Truth* and called *The Adventist Review and Sabbath Herald*. Now known as the *Adventist Review*, this magazine is more than 155 years old.

1852: James White began publishing a magazine for children and youth—*The Youth's Instructor*. This was the forerunner of *Insight* magazine.

1853: The first regular Sabbath schools were organized.

1860: The name Seventh-day Adventist was adopted.

School Starts

1853: A woman named Martha Byington started the first Adventist church school.

1872: First denominational school opened under G. H. Bell.

1874: Battle Creek College was established. It grew into Andrews University.

1882: Two church-sponsored secondary schools were created. These grew into Atlantic Union College and Pacific Union College. Adventist education was well on its way!

1896: Oakwood Industrial School opened near Huntsville, Alabama. It soon became the center for training Black leadership and eventually grew into Oakwood College.